Jesus and Prayer

Abena Safiyah Fosua

ABINGDON PRESS
Nashville

JESUS AND PRAYER

by Abena Safiyah Fosua

ISBN 13: 978-0-687-09071-6

07 08 09 10 11—10 9 8 7 6 5

MANUFACTURED IN THE UNITED STATES OF AMERICA

Contents

Meet the Writer 4
A Word of Welcome. 5
How to Use This Resource 6
1. The Habit of Prayer 7
2. Our Father in Heaven 19
3. Give Us This Day Our Daily Bread 33
4. Prayer Parables 45
5. Prayer and Healing 57
6. The John 17 Prayer 71
7. Prayer in the Garden of Gethsemane. 85
8. Prayers on the Cross 95

Abena Safiyah Fosua was born in Kansas City, Kansas. Her academic background includes a Bachelor of Arts degree from Northwestern University of Evanston, Illinois; coursework at the International Bible College of San Antonio, Texas; a Master of Divinity degree from Oral Roberts Seminary in Tulsa, Oklahoma; and a Doctor of Ministry degree from the United Theological Seminary of Dayton, Ohio, in Afrocentric Pastoring and Preaching. Dr. Fosua is an elder in the Greater New Jersey Annual Conference of The United Methodist Church.

Safiyah Fosua is recognized as a preacher who speaks to the soul of people. One of her sermons ("Talking to a Dead Man") appears in *The Wisdom of the Word-Faith: Great African-American Sermons* (Crown Publishers, 1996). Safiyua has written for Upper Room publications, Cokesbury's *Daily Bible Study*, and for Urban Ministries, Inc. Abingdon Press published her first book, *Mother Wit: 365 Meditations for African-American Women*, in the fall of 1996.

Safiyah Fosua is married to Kwasi I. Kena. The couple has two adult sons and one grandson. Before serving a term as missionaries with the General Board of Global Ministries, Safiyah and her husband were clergy members of the Iowa Annual Conference where, among other appointments, they served as the founding pastors of the Jubilee UMC in Waterloo. From 1996–2000, they served as commissioned GBGM missionaries in Ghana, West Africa, directing the Resource Development and Training Unit for the Methodist Church—Ghana. Currently, Safiyah serves as a General Board of Global Ministries missionary pastor in Asbury Park, New Jersey.

A Word of Welcome

Welcome to JESUS AND PRAYER, a study that helps you into the practice of prayer. This study examines several instances of prayer in the Bible, but more importantly, invites you to value and to try out your own prayers. Through this study you will

- Learn more about what prayer is.
- Examine what is arguably the best prayer for Christians for all time—the Lord's Prayer—petition by petition.
- Consider how Jesus taught his disciples about persistence in prayer as well as how to pray.
- Study how healing and prayer are related by studying Jesus' ministry of healing prayer.
- Participate in Jesus' prayer, often called the "High Priestly Prayer" for himself, the world, and his disciples through all time, including us.
- Gain greater insight into the person of Jesus Christ as he prayed in the garden of Gethsemane and from the cross.

This study gives you the opportunity not only to learn about prayer but also to pray in your own circumstances. It helps you understand the various elements of prayer and the sufficiency of prayer. You will also consider the import of what sometimes seems to be unanswered prayer, and how God works through even those seeming moments of silence to care for you.

We invite you to immerse yourself in the love of God through Christ as he prayed and worked and saved and loved humankind and to communicate your own needs and concerns in return. We pray that you will find a blessing in this study of prayer and in those for whom and with whom you pray.

How to Use This Resource

We hope you enjoy participating in this study, either on your own or with a group. We offer these hints and suggestions to make your study a success.

JESUS AND PRAYER is a self-contained study with all the teaching/learning suggestions conveniently located on or near the main text to which they refer. They are identified with the same heading (or a close abbreviation) as the heading in the main text. In addition to your Bible, all you need to have a successful group or individual study session is provided for you in this book.

Some special features are provided as well, such as the Bible 301 activities in the teaching helps. We usually think of the "101" designation as the beginning level; these "301" designations prompt you to dig deeper. In these instances you will be invited to look up Scriptures, key words, or concepts in the Bible dictionary, commentary, or atlas. On occasion, an added book or resource is cited that may be obtained from your local library or perhaps from your pastor. Those resources are extras; your study will be enriched by these added sources of information, but it is not dependent upon them.

This study is intentionally invitational. In the closing activity, you are invited to do three things: to give prayerful consideration to your relationship to Jesus Christ and make or renew your commitment, to offer your own spoken prayers, and to pray with and for others. We trust you will participate in these activities as you feel comfortable and that you will use them as a challenge to grow more confident in prayer and in your covenant with Jesus Christ.

Session One

This session focuses on the societal and cultural elements that shaped Jesus' life of habitual prayer.

Session Objective ■

Our objective is to understand how Jesus came to pray habitually and to consider ways we can develop a life of prayer and communion with God.

Session Preparation ■

Become acquainted with the beliefs and practices of at least two other religions that are observed in our country. Bring the following to the class session: several translations of the New Testament, a dictionary, and a Bible concordance.

Choose from among these activities and discussion starters to plan your lesson.

The Habit of Prayer ■

Look up the word *habit* in a dictionary. What kinds of things do you do without thinking about them? Read Luke 5:16 in as many Bible translations as you can find in your class-

The Habit of Prayer

"Jesus often withdrew to lonely places and prayed" (Luke 5:16, NIV)

What kinds of things do you do as often as possible? Luke 5:16 is one of several references Luke makes to Jesus praying. Other translations indicate that Jesus "often withdrew," "would often go," "from time to time would withdraw" to a private place to pray. These translations, considered together, lead us to conclude that, for Jesus, prayer was a habit.

We have been conditioned to think of habits in terms of actions that we want either to relinquish or to acquire. Dictionaries, however, define habits as customary manners or practices. The majority of contemporary psychologists have come to view habits as conditioned behavior over which one has little voluntary control. This suggests that we should think of habits, and particularly the habit of prayer, as customary actions rather than as extraordinary ones.

Stephen R. Covey, author of *The Seven Habits of Highly Effective People* (Simon and Schuster, 1989), defines *habit* as "the intersection of knowledge, skill, and desire." It can be said that Jesus was effective in prayer. He had practiced prayer often. As a Jew, he had been taught *how* to pray. He was driven by a *desire* to pray at every opportunity. Jesus knew why he was praying. Prayer was fundamental to his relationship with God.

room. What can you learn about Jesus' prayer life from the various ways that translators have chosen to render this verse? What methods have you used successfully either to form a new habit or break an old one?

Prayer and Jewish Culture ■

Pretend that you are describing Christian practices to a new believer. Which ones would you say are essential to Christianity?

Jewish prayers, rituals and sacrifices revealed the Jews' belief that they were indebted to God for everything. List at least three Christian prayers, rituals, or practices. What do they reveal about Christian beliefs?

Bible 301 ☐

As the world becomes increasingly "smaller," we are more likely to live among or work with people of other religious faiths. Describe the beliefs and religious practices of at least two different religious groups that you would encounter in your community or your state. How do they differ from Christian beliefs and practices? In what ways are they similar?

It came as no surprise to the Gospel writers that Jesus prayed often. Jesus did not introduce the concept of prayer. Jesus was born into a Jewish family, and prayer was an integral part of both Jewish faith and culture.

Prayer and Jewish Culture

Every aspect of Jewish life and culture is directed toward God. For the Jews of Jesus' day, religious practices, including prayer, were not an option or an aspiration, they were an *expectation*. Either alone, or in a group, Jews customarily said short prayers in the morning, the afternoon, and the evening in addition to prayer at "unscheduled" times throughout the day. Upon awakening and before going to sleep, they prayed the "Shema" taken from Deuteronomy 6:4-9. It was also customary to pray before and after meals.

Extensive prayers were a part of corporate worship at both Temple and synagogue. As a nation, Jews also observed holy days, such as the Day of Atonement, where praying and fasting were required. Jesus was nurtured in a culture that taught him the importance of prayer.

The people who lived in the nations surrounding Israel also had their own religious practices. They prayed—but for different reasons; and they prayed to their own gods. Prayer, for them, was frequently offered to coax an unwilling deity to deal favorably with them. Because the people of the surrounding nations did not feel loved by their gods, they often prayed in order to appease the gods' anger. Some devotees offered prayer and sacrifices in an effort to insure entrance into the afterlife.

The surrounding peoples usually chose to pray to *several* gods for favor and protection.

What are the differences between polytheism and monotheism? How might the polytheistic neighbors of the Hebrews have believed when their prayers to various gods were answered? How might they have interpreted a lack of response?

Answer to prayer is never guaranteed to be immediate or automatic. How did the Hebrew people recognize an answer to their prayers? What was distinctive about the way they prayed?

The Jews relied upon their relationship with God as the most important reason for praying. What is the most common motivation for Christian prayer? What role does your relationship with God play in your prayer life?

Explain how the rituals connected with Jewish law encouraged the development of prayer as a habit. Does Christian prayer also presuppose relationship with God?

The worship of many gods is known as *polytheism*. The surrounding cultures felt that each god had a limited domain. Their practices reveal that they might believe in one god for fertility, one for good crops, another for success in war, another for health, and the list could continue infinitely.

By contrast, the Jews practiced *monotheism*. This meant that they worshiped only one God. By Law, the Jews avoided any practice that would identify them with the worship of other gods. Important to our study, this also meant that all prayers were directed to the Almighty God who had been revealed to their ancestors—beginning with Abraham. They believed that God's reign extended over all things and that there was no other true god. The Jews believed that God had chosen them from among the nations because God loved them. God was in covenant with them: "I will be God to you and to your offspring after you" (Genesis 17:7). As a response to God's love and favor, they became a people who worshiped one God exclusively.

Jewish culture was structured to maintain its religious uniqueness. The law of Moses, held in reverence by every sect of Jews, served to keep Jews focused on their relationship with God. The laws concerning sacrifice dramatized the Jewish understanding that they were dependent upon God for everything: children, crops, possessions, even life itself. When sacrifices were offered, Jews often uttered spontaneous prayers asking for forgiveness, petitioning for God's favor, or expressing their desire for a better relationship with God.

It then follows that Jewish prayer presupposes relationship with God. So, when the Jews of Jesus' day prayed to keep the law, they were essentially praying for the ability to maintain their relationship with God. When they asked for forgiveness by offering prayers and sacrifices, they did so in hopes of re-establishing or strengthening a relationship that had been damaged by sin against God.

Jesus Learned to Pray as a Child

Religious education was another tool used in teaching subsequent generations how to maintain the Jews' unique relationship with God. In accordance with the law (see Deuteronomy 6:7-9), religious instruction began, for Jesus, in the home. We know that Jesus' earthly parents observed the law from the beginning of his life. On the eighth day of his life, he was circumcised and presented to the Lord in the Temple. A sacrifice was offered for him as the law prescribed (Leviticus 12:2-3, 6-8; Luke 2:21-24). We read that Mary and Joseph went to Jerusalem yearly for the Passover (Luke 2:41). We are safe in assuming that Jesus' family paid particular attention to his religious instruction because they were both aware that he was a child with a divine destiny (Luke 1:26-38; Matthew 1:20-21).

As a child, Jesus probably had been required to memorize the corporate prayers used by the Hebrew people in worship, the eighteen benedictions, or *berakoth*. Prayers, both memorized and spontaneous, were a natural accompaniment to the rituals and symbolic acts found in the life of the Jew.

The Psalms are sometimes referred to as Israel's prayer book. Many of the psalms were prayers that were said or sung on the sabbath or on other special days. Many devout Jews memorized them much like we memorize the Lord's Prayer. These psalms

Jesus Learned to Pray

Read Deuteronomy 6:6-9; 11:18-21. What do these passages teach us about the religious upbringing of Jewish children (at least the boys)?

Read Luke 1:26-38; 2:21-24, 41; Matthew 1:20-21; and Leviticus 12:2-3, 6-8 for an indication of how Jesus' earthly parents observed the law and understood their special child. Tell your own stories. Think about your earliest experiences with faith formation (even if you had no understanding at the time of what faith formation is). Who told you "God things"? How was this modeled (or not) in the life of those to whom you paid attention? How explicit was it to you that the faith community and the Bible had authority, support, and accountability for your well-being and upbringing? How do you continue this responsibility for the next generation?

As a child, what Christian creeds or confessions were you required to memorize? How did you learn to pray?

Hymns are one way to teach Christian doctrine. What is your favorite hymn? (Sing or read one or two of them together.) What does this hymn teach you about the Christian faith? Have you committed all or portions of your favorite hymns to memory?

Solitary Prayer ■

Form three groups to consider the three emphases of this section: prayer for refreshment, for focus, and for guidance. Look up the Scriptures in each of these emphases. Read surrounding verses as well to examine the context. For each of the Scripture passages, discuss: What was Jesus doing, why, and with whom? In what ways does Jesus' practice inform, form, or transform our lives? If you followed Jesus' practice faithfully, how might that change your life? In addition, talk about the questions indicated for each of the emphases.

Prayer for Refreshment ■

Jesus frequently sought opportunities to pray alone. Do you ever feel that you need to be alone to pray?

Do you have trouble finding a quiet place, time to go to a quiet place, or dealing with a time of quiet? (If so, you are not alone!) Brainstorm with others how

called the nation to righteousness, rehearsed God's mighty acts in the life of Israel, or anticipated the reign of God. Jesus made frequent references to the psalms when he taught.

Solitary Prayer

"In the morning, while it was still very dark, [Jesus] got up and went out to a deserted place, and there he prayed" (Mark 1:35).

Thus far, much of our emphasis has been upon the public, or corporate, prayers of Israel. During the time of Christ, devout Jews also prayed individually at various times throughout the day. The disciples had frequent opportunity to observe how Jesus prayed privately. He was often found "stealing away" to a deserted place or to a mountain to pray.

We learn several things from the solitary prayer life of Christ.

Solitary prayer provides an opportunity for refreshment. As Jesus' popularity grew, he increasingly was forced to contend with the demands of the crowds. Mark 1:37 alludes to this press of people: "Everyone is searching for you." The crowds wanted to hear Jesus' profound teaching; many wanted him to touch and heal them; and others wanted advice. Those persons who do disaster relief work bear witness to the short amount of time it takes to reach a stage of burnout. No doubt, a time apart for prayer was also a time of rest: "Come away to a deserted place all by yourselves and rest a while" (Mark 6:31).

It does not, however, take intense work with distressed people to prove our need for

to overcome those difficulties. If time for reflection in a quiet place is easy or natural for you, what suggestions can you offer someone else to help establish this practice? How does it help and refresh you? How did you go about setting this practice in place for yourself?

Take five minutes to be quiet, in a private place if possible, to pray or to write in a journal about one special prayer concern.

Prayer for Focus

Jesus found it necessary to get away from the noise and clamor of the crowds in order to stay focused. Does our culture make allowances for our needs for solitude or prayer, or even for time to think? What adjustments would you have to make in order to pray alone for one-half day? to have time at the beginning and/or end of each day to think and pray about what is ahead or has happened and compare it to your goals and needs for the day?

Prayer for Guidance

How do you perceive answers to prayer? What discernment practices have you found effective and how do you know they have "worked"? What might happen if church administrative boards or councils paused for an evening of prayer before making major ministry-related decisions?

times apart with God. Daily life in this high-tech era presents enough challenges and pressures to prove our need for periodic times of solitary prayer. Being alone with God provides an opportunity for each of us to hear God and receive the restoration that we need to be effectively present for one another. Henri Nouwen says in *Reaching Out: The Three Movements of the Spiritual Life* (Doubleday, 1975): "Solitude does not pull us away from our fellow human beings but instead makes real fellowship possible."

Solitary prayer provides an opportunity for focus. Have you ever made an unwise decision when you were caught up in the moment or carried away with the momentum? The Gospel of John reports such a time when the crowds were so impressed with the miraculous feeding of the 5,000 that they were going to make Jesus king by force (John 6:14-15). In light of the politics of that time, this action would have provoked the Romans and probably led to great bloodshed. Jesus responded to their misplaced enthusiasm by sending his disciples to the other side of the Sea of Galilee and retreating to the mountains to pray (Matthew 14:22-23; Mark 6:45-46; John 6:15-17). Jesus knew that his kingdom would be of a different nature and that this was not his time to be their king.

Solitary prayer provides an opportunity to receive guidance. Luke, the historian, reports that Jesus spent the entire night alone in prayer before announcing his choice of twelve disciples (Luke 6:12-16). Gospel history might have been quite different without this night of solitude and prayer.

Consider these questions about the early monastic tradition and how it might work today. Why did the first monks go to the desert? What do people do when they go to the desert? Do spiritual retreats provide a short-term opportunity to experience the solitude that monks sought in the desert? Is it possible to retreat to the desert symbolically without leaving home? Give some explanation for each of your responses.

There are many ways to separate oneself for prayer, and some of these ways involve physicality. Consider taking time now or later to pray using a labyrinth. (See, for example, *www.gracecathedral.org/lab yrinth* or *www.lessons4living.com*.) Or, explore how dance, chanting, drumming, or other repetitive motion can enhance breath prayer or other meditative prayer.

Should We All Go to the Desert to Pray?

Near the end of the third century, a young Egyptian man named Anthony was impressed by the teaching found in Matthew 19:21, which told a rich man to sell his possessions and give them to the poor in order to have treasures in heaven. Anthony did just that and retreated to the desert to devote the rest of his life to prayer and solitude. Ironically, he was not alone for long, because a number of people soon followed him looking for instruction. He devoted several years to instructing these disciples in what came to be known as the monastic life. Since that time, untold numbers of men and women have forsaken their own ambitions and retreated to deserts and remote places for solitary prayer.

The monastic movement, as it is sometimes called, has not been without its problems. Some, for example, only went to the desert to escape having to deal with people. Of this, noted monastic Thomas Merton said in *New Seeds of Contemplation* (Abbey of Gethsemani, Inc., 1961), "Go into the desert not to escape other men but in order to find them in God." By this, he implied that the purpose of solitary prayer is not just to get away from people and the evils of society but also to gain the vision and the focus necessary to return from the desert and work toward a just and godly society.

The monastic movement often raises serious issues for the rest of us. Are we, somehow, less spiritual if we have not chosen a life of prayer and solitude? In response to this question, consider viewing solitary prayer in symbolic rather than literal terms. Those who retreated to the deserts for prayer ultimately wanted to pray more sincerely and thereby to please God. We do not have to leave our jobs or our families to pray more sincerely or to please God. We can do both where we are.

The desert can come to symbolize the spiritual discipline through which we turn our thoughts and attention away from the din and clatter of life. Doing so frees us to reach instead for God, who yearns to speak to the hearts of women and men—whenever we are available to listen.

Prayer on the Mountaintop

"After he had dismissed the crowds, he went up the mountain by himself to pray" (Matthew 14:23).

The Gospels report that Jesus often prayed for long periods of time in the mountains. Luke 6:12 tells us that he continued all night in prayer. Mark 6:48 tells us that Jesus was praying into the fourth watch of the night ("early in the morning"), which would have been from 3:00 to 6:00 A.M. These reports served to connect him with the historic tradition of the Jewish prophets who were also known to spend a great deal of time in prayer—often in the mountains. Consider, for example, the many accounts of Moses on the mountain. God was initially revealed to Moses at a mountain (Exodus 3). The Law was given to the Israelites from Mount Sinai, also called Horeb (Exodus 19–20). The mountain was also the place where Moses met with God for long seasons of prayer or intercession.

Elijah, another Old Testament prophet, called the nation back to monotheism on a mountain. Earlier in Israel's history, the Israelites had regressed to offering sacrifices

Prayer on the Mountaintop ■

Read Mark 6:46 and Luke 6:12. Jesus frequently prayed well into the night. What motivated him to this practice? What do you think it accomplished? Is it necessary for modern Christians to pray for long periods of time? Why or why not?

Bible 301 □

Using a concordance, find the instances where Jesus is in the mountains either for prayer or for ministry. What does the frequency of Jesus' times apart suggest or model for you in your own prayer life?

Read Exodus 3:9-10. How does Moses' experience at the holy mountain inform your own practice of prayer?

In small groups, divide these selected passages: 1 Kings 11:4-13; 18:20-40; and 19:1-18. Compare

Elijah's prayer to those of the prophets of Baal. What do we learn about the beliefs of each from their prayers? How does Elijah's experience *after* the contest on Mt. Carmel demonstrate human strength and frailty in our faith and prayer life? Describe a time when your experience paralleled Elijah's. How did you feel? What did you do?

Bible 301 ☐

Using a concordance, look for references to "high places." List instances when the Hebrews offered sacrifices to foreign gods on these high places. What do we learn about human nature from these accounts?

Read Deuteronomy 11:26-29; Deuteronomy 27:11-13; 2 Kings 17:24-28, 41; and John 4:20. Who were the Samaritans? Why did the Samaritans choose this mountain as an alternative to worshiping at the Temple in Jerusalem?

Locate Mt. Gerazim and Jerusalem on a Bible atlas or map in your study Bible.

Locate an encyclopedia article or an Internet page describing the importance of Mt. Olympus in Greek and Roman mythology. Compare this with the importance of mountains and mountaintop activity described in the Scriptures you have read. Does our culture have any popular

to false gods on the mountains. These were known as high places. (See, for example, the sad account of Solomon's idolatry in 1 Kings 11:4-13.) Elijah's famous challenge to the prophets of Baal took place on Mount Carmel (1 Kings 18:20-40). After a particularly discouraging time in ministry, God was revealed to Elijah on Mount Horeb (1 Kings 19:8). Elisha, Elijah's successor, could often be found on Mount Carmel. Common belief holds that a school of the prophets was established there. Those who believed that Jesus was at least a prophet, if not the Messiah, undoubtedly referred to his prayer habits as proof.

Mountains were also significant for the Samaritans. When the Assyrians conquered Israel, the Hebrew elite were carried off into exile. The remaining peasants and artisans were assimilated with the incoming Assyrians and other conquered peoples who emigrated there. The Samaritans were descendants of Jews who had intermarried with non-Jews during the Assyrian captivity (see 2 Kings 17:24-28, 41). When the exiles returned to rebuild Jerusalem, they considered the Samaritans religious infidels who were unfit to be numbered among them. The Samaritans who had religious roots in Hebrew tradition recalled the blessing ceremony from Deuteronomy 11:29 and 27:12 and chose Mount Gerizim as their new place of worship.

The surrounding cultures of Jesus' day also believed that mountains were places where mere mortals encountered the divine. One has only to mention Mt. Olympus, the home of Zeus and Jupiter in the Greco-Roman cultures. So, for the non-Jew, the mountain was a place where they believed the gods could be found.

beliefs or superstitions about mountains? How do popular, or folk, beliefs like these influence Christian beliefs?

This frequent mention of prayer in the mountains reinforces the fact that Jesus lived in divine fellowship with God. This symbolism enabled many of the Jews of his day to accept him as a prophet and later, for some, as Messiah. The mountains also held significance for the Samaritans and for the Gentiles because of their religious encounters and theophanies (God's self-revelation to persons) in the mountains.

Historic ■ Applications

Read 1 Thessalonians 5:17; Romans 12:12; and Colossians 4:2. What do you learn from these verses about prayer in the early Christian church? What encouragement do you receive and give to your faith community to be regular and persistent in prayer? How does (or might) such encouragement help?

Consider Brother Lawrence's habit of constant prayer and then experiment yourself in praying without ceasing over two weeks (or whatever trial period you choose). Start small and build each day; for example, commit to a time of constant prayer for ten minutes twice a day for two days, then twenty minutes twice a day for two days, and so on. Keep a journal of your experience and review at the end of your trial period to see what obstacles you encountered, how you dealt with them, and what you accomplished. What

Historic Applications

The fact that prayer was a natural habit for Jesus has profound implications for us today. Perhaps you are already familiar with the Pauline injunction to "pray without ceasing" (1 Thessalonians 5:17). How do we live in this modern world *and* pray without ceasing? The Christian church has wrestled for centuries with the dilemma of practicing habitual prayer.

Notable among these faithful Christians struggling with the meaning and practice of prayer was Brother Lawrence. Brother Lawrence lived in a monastery where prayers were recited at established times of the day either in community or in private. As one devoted to a life of prayer, however, he was concerned that he was not praying in between those times. He took seriously the Pauline injunction to pray without ceasing. Over time, he developed the practice of praying while he worked in the monastery's kitchen as well as at any idle time when he was aware that he was not praying. As a result, for him, prayer became a habit. Eventually, he said that for him, there was no difference between the time of business and the time of prayer. "While several persons are at the same time calling for different things, I possess God in as great tranquillity

adjustments, if any, did you have to make to pray while doing your work?

Consider using the Jesus Prayer for your prayer experiment. Or, write a one-sentence prayer of just a few words or identify a musical phrase or stanza that could be used in place of the Jesus Prayer. We are also faced with difficulties in praying while pursuing daily occupations. Make a list of practical methods that any person could use to remember to pray more frequently.

Do you ever find yourself daydreaming while reciting a memorized prayer? Do you think that daydreaming is an unwanted distraction or a natural result of prayer?

How would you describe the difference between the habit of prayer, the ritual of prayer, and rote prayer? How can you focus your prayer life for the greatest investment and meaning for you and your relationship with God?

An Invitation to Prayer

Learning to pray habitually is more than just remembering to pray often. It is

as if I were on my knees at the blessed sacrament" (*The Practice of the Presence of God*, Fleming H. Revell Company, 1958).

The Jesus Prayer is another vehicle for learning the habit of prayer. It was used extensively in the sixth century and revived in the Eastern (Orthodox) Church in the fourteenth century. It involves the repetition of a sentence prayer based on Luke 18:13: "Lord Jesus Christ, Son of God, have mercy on me, a sinner."

The Jesus Prayer was popularized in the Eastern Church after the publication of a small book known as *The Way of a Pilgrim*. In that book, an anonymous monk tells the story of a man who asked a *starets* (spiritual father) how to pray without ceasing. The *starets*, in response, explained the Jesus Prayer and invited him to pray the prayer "first 3,000 times a day, then 6,000 times, and finally 12,000 times" (*The Jesus Prayer*, St. Vladimir's Seminary Press, 1987). This resulted in the man beginning to pray with every breath. The increasing number of books on the Jesus Prayer testifies to the renewed interest that modern Christians have shown in this prayer.

For centuries, Christians have employed any number of techniques and rituals in an effort to learn how to pray as a habit. Many people have drawn closer to God through the use of these novel approaches to prayer. Unfortunately, Christian history has also proven that it is far too easy for us to emphasize the rituals while forgetting the reasons for prayer.

An Invitation to Prayer

Prayer for Jesus and his disciples was much more than reciting memorized phrases at the appropriate times of day. Prayer, for becoming aware of our connection to God and making a conscious effort to keep that connection ever before us. When you pray, are you aware of being connected to God?

them, was more than a laundry list of wants and needs. It was conscious, intentional, communion with the Living God.

More than any of us, Jesus lived with a constant awareness of his connection to God. Consider this study an invitation to become more aware of God's presence in your own lives by examining Jesus' life of prayer. Hear what he said to his disciples when he taught them what we have come to know as the Lord's Prayer. Listen to the prayers of the saints around him. Reflect upon what he taught the disciples about prayer and healing. Celebrate Christian unity as we examine what is often called the High Priestly Prayer of John 17. Struggle with the prayers that flow from Gethsemane experiences. Take yet another look at Jesus' dying words. As we reflect prayerfully upon the many facets of Jesus' life of prayer, may our own prayers multiply and increase in depth.

Closing Prayer

As you close in prayer, thank God for the relationship into which you have been called. Ask for the grace to be ever mindful that you are in constant living fellowship with the Almighty God.

Preparation for Next Week

Consider keeping a prayer journal. During this coming week, note the ease and frequency of your prayers. At the end of one week, covenant with God and a spiritual mentor to increase the *quality* of your prayer life.

Session Two

Our Father in Heaven

Session Focus ■
This session focuses on the first half of the Lord's Prayer with particular attention being given to its social and historical context.

Session Objective ■
The objective of this session is to gain a deeper understanding of the principles found in the first half of the Lord's Prayer: relationship, God in human imagery, hallowing God's name, and the kingdom of God.

Session Preparation ■
Locate several versions of the Lord's Prayer, including ones in your denominational book of worship. Bring copies of these versions of the Lord's Prayer to the session.

Choose from among these activities and discussion starters to plan your lesson.

Our Father in Heaven ■
How old were you when you learned the Lord's Prayer? When are we supposed to pray the Lord's Prayer?

For about two thousand years, Christians of all denominations have committed to memory the words of the Lord's Prayer. References to the Lord's Prayer can be found in the *Didache*, the oldest known book of church instruction outside of the New Testament canon, written between A.D. 120–180 and intended for Gentile Christians. In the *Didache*, or the *Teaching of the Twelve Apostles*, the author writes: "And do not pray as the wicked [do]; pray instead this way, as the Lord directed in his gospel" (Didache 8:2). The prayer closely follows Matthew's Gospel.

The Lord's Prayer, or the prayer that Jesus taught his disciples, continues to be found in prayer books and orders of worship all over the world. The Lord's Prayer has been translated into thousands of local languages. Where did the Lord's Prayer originate?

A Model for Prayer
The Lord's Prayer as we know it can be found in both Matthew and Luke's Gospels, but its roots are in the Hebrew prayer forms of the synagogue. Jesus' prayer is similar to a summary of the Eighteen Benedictions, the standing prayers that made up the central ritual of the synagogue service.

A quick comparison of the two Gospel accounts reveals slight differences in the wording. These do not imply contradiction.

A Model for Prayer

Compare Matthew 6:9-13 to Luke 11:1-4. What differences do you note? How do these two versions of the Lord's Prayer differ from the one you first memorized?

Think about how you say the Lord's Prayer. Is it by rote or are you conscious of each attribution and petition and what they mean? How does this prayer empower you? model for you what Jesus wants you to pray?

A Negative Example

Read Matthew 6:5-6. Jesus condemned the public prayers of the Pharisees when they used their prayers to impress people. How would you define what it means to pray like a hypocrite? Give one or two examples.
Are you impressed by those who pray well publicly? How comfortable are you praying aloud in front of someone else? a small group? a large group? Some persons are very reluctant to pray before others because they think their prayers are not "pretty" enough. Is there a wrong way to pray a sincere prayer? Is there a right way to pray an insincere prayer? Explain your answer. What kinds of things do we learn about a person by listening to his or her public prayers?

Modern scholars, pointing to the minor differences between Matthew's account and Luke's account, suggest that the Lord's Prayer is really a *summary* of the prayer principles that Jesus taught.

Many are surprised to learn that Jesus probably never intended for this prayer to be used ritualistically, or as an amulet in times of danger as is often portrayed in the movies. It was, instead, intended to be a model for both public and private prayer.

Teaching by Negative Example

In Matthew's account (Matthew 6:9-13), the Lord's Prayer is given in the context of the Sermon on the Mount. Jesus began earlier in this chapter by teaching his disciples how they should *not* pray: "And whenever you pray, do not be like the hypocrites; for they love to stand and pray in the synagogues and at the street corners, so that they may be seen by others" (Matthew 6:5).

The hypocrites referred to in this passage were Pharisees who Jesus had found to be religiously arrogant. The sect of the Pharisees began as a religious restorative movement in the Jewish faith. They had intended to call the nation back to the correct observance of the law of Moses, from which Israel had strayed. They intended to do so by spelling out, in detailed ways, how to pray, observe laws of cleanliness, and observe other rituals and laws of holiness. Over time, the beautiful symbolism of the law became for some of them showy, excessive rituals.

To give an example from Christ's day, the Pharisees were known to stop wherever they were to observe prescribed prayer times. In doing so, they were frequently found praying aloud conspicuously in the marketplaces or

Why did Jesus encourage his disciples to pray in secret? What do you think "in secret" means here? How does this reconcile with Jesus' earlier teaching to "let your light shine" (Matthew 5:14-16)?

Are you most comfortable praying at church in unison with the congregation, privately during quiet moments of the worship service, in a small prayer group, with a prayer partner, or at home alone? Why? Does the purpose of prayer change, depending on the setting? Why or why not?

Read Matthew 6:7. Why does Jesus speak against the long repetitive prayers of the Gentiles? What positive underlying prayer principle do you think Jesus is attempting to illustrate here?

In light of the negative examples of public praying, what guidelines would you suggest for praying publicly? for praying at all?

How can we guard against public or private prayer becoming empty ritual or nothing more than piled up words?

on the street corners. A nineteenth-century Bible commentator, Alfred Edersheim, reports that one would bend so low "that every vertebra in his back would stand out separate," or at least till "the skin over his heart would fall into folds" (*Sketches of Jewish Social Life*, 1876, Christian Classics Ethereal Library).

Personal piety could be lost in the backwash of shoddy public performances. A movement that began with honorable intentions sometimes lost its way in emphasizing rule and ritual over justice and holiness. When the Pharisees' meticulous observance of the letter of their own laws overshadowed the real spirit of the law of Moses, which was to keep the people in vital relationship with God and in just relationship with neighbor, Jesus was vocal and critical. Regrettably, the word *Pharisee* eventually became a synonym for dogmatic practices and hypocrisy. We, too, can become "pharisaic" if we forget the true reason for prayer—our relationship with God and neighbor.

Jesus also took issue with having the wrong purpose for prayer. "When you are praying," he cautioned, "do not heap up empty phrases as the Gentiles do; for they think that they will be heard because of their many words" (Matthew 6:7).

This injunction does not mean that we should not pray about the same issue more than once, or that we cannot repeat ourselves when praying. Jesus himself prayed about the same thing several times in the garden of Gethsemane (Matthew 26:44). Scripture also records that the apostle Paul prayed repeatedly about a problem (2 Corinthians 12:7-9). We are warned against praying like the Gentiles do.

Gentiles, who worshiped other gods, often

Read 1 Kings 18 and Acts 19. How do the prayers to Baal and Diana contrast with prayers to God? What is the purpose of repeating the same prayer requests if we grant that God hears prayers the first time? How do you think repeated prayers affect God? the person who prays?

babbled the same phrases or petitions over and over, as if the repetition improved the efficacy of the prayer or the attempt could weary their gods into answering. For an example of this practice look at the prophets of Baal in 1 Kings 18:26 or the worshipers of the goddess Diana in Ephesus who yelled her name for two hours (Acts 19:34).

Unlike the peoples who surrounded Israel, we do not pray to keep God happy, to avoid God's anger, or to manipulate God to grant our demands. Neither do we pray just to present our ever-expanding list of requests for special favor, to fulfill duty, or to work our way to heaven. We pray because we are connected to God and because we need to pray.

The Disciples' Request

The Disciples' Request

Read Luke 9:51-62 as an indicator of the context in which the disciples asked Jesus for a lesson in prayer; then read Luke 11:1-4. No doubt the disciples already knew the synagogue prayers. Why would they need lessons from Jesus? What, if anything, has prompted you to evaluate your need to pray and your need for instruction in prayer?

Luke's shorter account of the Lord's Prayer (Luke 11:2-4) places it in an entirely different context. Luke's purpose here is to instruct his faith community in the ways of Jesus by having Jesus model particular behaviors. In Luke's Gospel, the Lord's Prayer was Jesus' response to a request: "Lord, teach us to pray, as John taught his disciples" (Luke 11:1b). Luke has already written that Jesus' "days drew near for him to be taken up" so he, along with his disciples, "set his face to go to Jerusalem" (9:51) with all the tribulation that would follow. Knowing how to pray, and subsequently to remain in the will of God, would be important for the disciples in this circumstance.

It was a common Jewish practice for great teachers and leaders of prayer to compose a short set prayers. These prayers were thought to capture the teacher's concept of ideal piety toward God. Those who studied under great teachers often learned their teacher's prayer. It is apparent, from the pas-

Who have been your prayer teachers? With what aspect(s) of prayer would you like help? Who would you identify as great teachers and leaders of prayer today?

sage, that John's disciples, following this practice, had learned his personal prayers. Now, Jesus' disciples were making what would be considered a normal request of their teacher, *Lord teach us to pray.*

Structure of the Prayer ■

When you are preparing to pray, do you form a mental outline? What kinds of things go in the first part of your prayers? What determines the order of your prayer concerns?

Structure of the Prayer

The Lord's Prayer itself can be divided conveniently into two halves. After the invocation, "Our Father," the first half of the prayer contains petitions directed toward God and concern God's *name*, God's *kingdom*, and God's *will*. The second half of the prayer, which we will examine in the next chapter, deals with our needs: provisions, forgiveness, and deliverance from temptations and trials. The prayer concludes with a doxology or expression of praise to God: For "the kingdom and the power and the glory are yours forever. Amen." In this chapter, let us take a closer look at the first half of the Lord's Prayer.

Relationship ■

What is your favorite address to God? Why?

The Jews, as an entire nation, saw themselves in relationship with God. Look up Exodus 4:22; Deuteronomy 14:1; 32:26; and Isaiah 63:16. What blessings, privileges, and responsibilities come with being a child of God? Do you perceive yourself as a child of God? Is this concept a personal or intellectual one? What does this mean to you, day by day? How does the concept of

A Prayer Based on Relationship

How shall we approach God in prayer? What words are appropriate for invocation when addressing the eternal God, who is Spirit (John 4:24; 2 Corinthians 3:17)? Jesus taught, "When you pray, say: Father . . ." (Luke 11:2).

The use of the title "father" grounds the prayer in Israel's corporate relationship with God. Since the time that God sent Moses to confront Pharaoh, Israel had, as a people, been known as the children of God (Exodus 4:22; Deuteronomy 14:1; 32:6; and Isaiah 63:16).

Though the imagery of God as Father is found frequently in Hebrew Scriptures, the Jews did not appear to be in the habit of using the term *Father* as an invocation in

being a child of God affect the way that you either relate to God or pray to God?

Does America have a similar relationship with God? Are there other nations that can be said to have a *corporate* relationship with God?

Look up these passages and their context in Matthew, Luke, John, Romans, Galatians, and First John. What do these verses teach us about our relationship with God? Which name for God best expresses the reality of your personal relationship with God?

God in Human Terms ■

Imagine that you are teaching a class in vacation Bible school. Most of the children in your class do not attend any church. One particular child, who has

prayer. Some suggest that this metaphor may have been avoided in the Old Testament because the Hebrews' Near Eastern neighbors used the terms in fertility rites that carried sexual overtones. Within the Greco-Roman philosophies, Zeus was also considered a parent figure, as in Cleanthes's hymn to Zeus that claims humankind to be "born of you" and sharing "in the likeness of deity." Perhaps this is why Matthew, in writing to a Jewish audience, chose the phrase *Father, who lives in the heavens* to distinguish the Almighty God from the local gods.

The use of the word *father* also grounds prayer in our personal relationship with God. When Jesus came on the scene, his Jewish detractors must have been disturbed by the ways in which he alluded to the fatherhood of God. From his baptism to the Mount of Transfiguration, heaven acknowledged him as the Son of God (Matthew 3:17 and Matthew 17:5). Jesus himself repeatedly addressed and made reference to God as his Father (see, for example Matthew 7:21; John 8:28; or Luke 22:42). When Jesus prayed, he did so fully aware of his relationship to God. In teaching us to address God in prayer by using parental terminology, he affirms that we are also children of God. Later, New Testament writers repeatedly affirmed and reminded believers that we are indeed children of God (see Romans 8:15-16; Galatians 3:26; and 1 John 3:1).

Imagining God in Human Terms

Jesus began his instructive prayer with the term *Father*. In doing so, he used an *anthropomorphism* (a human reference or image to talk about something nonhuman), in this case, God. When we hear phrases such as "the eyes of the Lord," we are not invited to

shown great interest in your class, asks you, "What does God look like?" What will you say to this child?

Brainstorm all the images of God from Scripture that you can think of (human or not). Which images provide helpful insights to you about the nature of God?

Consider the various ways that people have described Jesus Christ in art, music, literature, or other art form. Choose one medium and use it to create an image of God that speaks to you. (Have on hand various art supplies.) Show your creation, then discuss the challenges that would arise if God were described without using any human imagery.

visualize a God with eyes like ours but rather to grasp the notion that God has ways of seeing and knowing.

As human beings, our perception of spiritual things is limited. It is natural for us to want to use human imagery to conceptualize certain attributes of God. However, when we use such imagery, we also run the risk of distorting or limiting our understandings of God. God cannot be bound by or confined to our human point of reference.

The Scripture, in fact, uses both male and female imagery in an attempt to describe the breadth and depth of God. Isaiah 49:14-15 and Luke 13:34, for example, allude to God as a mother figure. Yet, regardless of how many or what type of images we use, no words can adequately convey the fullness of who God is or what God does. Just as we human beings cannot be fully defined by our physical characteristics, personality, or accomplishments, God cannot be defined by comparison to any human image.

Human imagery can, however, be seen as a springboard to spiritual insight. Jesus' invitation to approach God as we would a loving nurturing parent is also an invitation to see ourselves, male and female, created in the image of God (Genesis 1:27).

Hallowed Be Your Name

Hallowed Be Your Name

Discuss the various ways in which you have heard the name of God used this week. To what extent is God's name "hallowed" or kept holy in contemporary society?

Hallowed is a peculiar word with Middle English origins that has fallen into disuse. Its root, *hallow*, means "to set aside for sacred use, or to make holy." Another way of saying this sentence might be, "May your name be kept holy," or "May your name be honored."

This prayer petition has its origin in the third commandment (Exodus 20:7), which exhorts us to consider God's name sacred and to avoid using it in vain. Considered in this light, the use of *Father* in the invocation can also be seen as another way of "hallowing" God's name.

Bible 301 ☐

Read Exodus 20:7. Use a Bible dictionary look up the names for God, including Adonai, El Shaddai, and YHWH. What insights about God do you gain from these honorific names? Which names of God do we use to promote the concept of "hallowing" God's name today?

Names of God

The Hebrews used various appellations of God to keep this commandment. For example, when reading Scripture aloud, the word Adonai *or* Lord *was substituted for* Yahweh *(properly* YHWH*), the covenant name for God in the Old Testament. Frequently the Jews used honorific names reflecting God's attributes or relationship with Israel like El Shaddai, probably meaning in Hebrew "God, the One of the Mountains" and translated from the Septuagint (the Greek Old Testament) as "Almighty God" (see Genesis 17:1) or the "God of Abraham" (see Genesis 31:42 or 1 Chronicles 29:18). When writing of God, only the consonants YHWH were used so that the reader might avoid accidentally speaking the name of God aloud. These four consonants are also known as the Tetragrammaton and are used instead of* Yahweh *to show the proper respect both to God and to the Jewish worshiper who keeps faith with the commandment to hallow God's name.*

Of Kings and Kingdoms ■

Read 1 Samuel 8 for background on the establishment of the kingship in Israel. What was at stake? What was the price?

Of Kings and Kingdoms

Kings and kingdoms would have been familiar imagery to the disciples. The judge Samuel, living over ten centuries earlier, had been petitioned and coaxed by the people to appoint a king over them. Samuel was insulted and outraged on God's behalf; nevertheless he prayed about this concern (1 Samuel 8:4-9). God acquiesced but warned of the consequences of anointing a king who would take the best of what they had (8:10-18). Saul became the first king, inaugurating nearly six centuries of monarchy. This desire reflected more than just the desire for a temporal king; it further represented a rejection of God as true king (8:7).

Bible 301 ☐

Using a Bible dictionary, look up "kingship," "Herod," "Judas Maccabeus," and "Rome." Summarize how all these factors and persons coalesced to forge the religious and political climate of first-century Palestine.

How do you, or would you, feel about someone having unlimited authority or reign over you? With no monarch in this country, how can Christians in the United States develop an appreciation for the sovereignty of God? What are the personal implications involved with inviting God to be your Sovereign God?

During the Roman occupation, praying for any other kingdom to come was radical and possibly risky. Are there any kingdoms that are challenged today when we pray the Lord's Prayer? If so, how? How are the tiny kingdoms we set up for ourselves challenged?

A Brief History

Throughout centuries of both heroic and villainous kings, the people of God did hold a vision of God as the ultimate ruler whose kingdom was not only of this earth. In the sixth century B.C., governance of Palestine fell into the hands of a succession of conquering nations who effectively abolished the lineage of Israelite and Judahite kings. Following the Maccabean revolt in the mid-160's B.C., the Jews finally regained a short-lived national freedom for the first time in about four hundred years. Idumea (or Edom), south of Judea, had also been dominated by a series of conquering nations. During this brief period of sovereignty, the Jews subjugated Idumea and forced the Jewish faith on them. In a reversal of Judea's fortune, Rome gained control over the entire area in 63 B.C. Herod, appointed king in 40, spent about three years solidifying his rule over the intractable Judeans, finally capturing Jerusalem in 37 B.C.

When the Romans took power in Palestine, they imposed the reign of their emperor, titled Caesar, over their new subjects and expected allegiance to his authority. Open opposition to Rome or its Caesar often merited the death penalty by crucifixion. The Romans placed a Roman sympathizer, Herod, on Israel's throne. Herod was by birth an Idumean and nominally Jewish, as a product of his earlier "conversion." His leadership openly antagonized the Jews, especially since he was a self-interested and bloodthirsty political puppet. In the context of this abominable political situation, the Jews hoped for both a better temporal kingdom and for the reign of their eternal King.

Which Kingdom Do You Mean?

When Jesus taught his disciples to pray, "thy Kingdom come," he engaged them on both the earthly and eternal understandings of the kingdom of God. Both Jesus and John the Baptist frequently referred to this coming Kingdom in their preaching (see, for example, Matthew 3:1-2, 14-15). Both preached entrance into this Kingdom by repentance. Repeatedly, Jesus taught that the time of the Kingdom's full realization could not be predicted (see Matthew 24:36, 42; 25:13; Mark 13:32; and Acts 1:7). Yet, Jesus frequently referred to present manifestations of this Kingdom (see Matthew 12:28; Luke 10:8-11; and 11:20).

The kingdom of God is the same as the kingdom of Heaven. In an attempt to keep the third Commandment concerning the improper use of the Lord's name, some Jews substituted the word *heaven* for God (see Luke 15:18, 21 or Mark 11:30 for other examples).

What kind of kingdom did the Jewish disciples have in mind when Jesus instructed them to pray that God's kingdom would come on earth as it is in heaven? The majority of the Jews embraced belief in a long-awaited ruler after the figure of David—who would be their king (Jeremiah 30:9; Ezekiel 37:24). This figure came to be understood as the Anointed One, or Messiah (Daniel 9:25).

Jews of Jesus' day held at least two major views about the *nature* of this coming Kingdom. For some, the kingdom of God would be one where the Jews would, once

---

Which Kingdom? ■

How do you think a person enters the kingdom of God?

In three small groups, divide and then look up the Scripture references in this first paragraph. How is the Kingdom understood in the passage? How do you understand the presence and the "not-yet-ness" of the Kingdom?

What manifestations of God's kingdom are apparent today?

Read Isaiah 9:2-7; Jeremiah 30:9; Ezekiel 37:24; Daniel 9:25; and Zechariah 9:9-17 to study who and what the Hebrews expected of their long-awaited deliverer. How are these expectations both earthly and eternal?

The zealots anticipated a political kingdom and worked to overthrow the Romans. If you learned that modern Christian zealots were plotting to overthrow a repressive government in another country, what would be your response?

Look up the Scriptures on this page and describe in your own words (1) the kingdom of God as a spiritual kingdom; (2) the kingdom of God that has already come; (3) the kingdom of God as a future kingdom that will bring God's greatest blessings and will bring human history to a close. What do you have in mind when you pray for God's kingdom to come?

What do the ministries of your church reveal about your congregation's beliefs concerning the kingdom of God? Discuss how each interpretation of the kingdom of God would influence the kind of ministries that the church as a whole does as well as ministries that local congregations do. For example, if the leaders in a local congregation believed that the kingdom of God is a spiritual kingdom, what kind of ministries would you expect to find there?

again, rule themselves. *Zealots,* a Jewish sect anticipating a political kingdom, worked actively to resist and overthrow the Romans, even if it meant suffering and death. Those in power viewed some of Jesus' activities as those of a zealot, citing his controversial choice of disciples and his triumphal entrance into Jerusalem as proof. These were among the accusations that eventually led to Jesus' crucifixion as a political rebel. He was charged with conspiring to overthrow the government (Luke 23:1-2; John 19:12-16).

Other Jews anticipated the coming of an *eschatological* or future kingdom that would bring history to a close. Support for this interpretation of the kingdom of God was readily found in passages like Zechariah 14:5-9 and Daniel 7:13-14. According to this interpretation, the Son of Man would come, the Final Judgment would take place, and God's reign would be established on earth. Jesus' discourses in Matthew 7:21-23; 8:11-12; and 25:31-46 could readily have been applied to this understanding of the coming Kingdom.

What do we modern Christians have in mind when we pray for God's kingdom to come? Some of us believe that the kingdom of God is a *spiritual kingdom,* using Luke 17:20-21 ("the kingdom of God is *within* you") to support the view that God's reign takes place in the human heart. A better rendering of that passage is *"among* you," signifying that the kingdom of God has already come because Christ has come, pointing to the past and present works of Christ as evidence (see Matthew 12:28).

Another popular belief about the kingdom of God says that the greatest blessings of God's kingdom are yet to be realized. Here, passages like the parable of the ten bridesmaids and other discourses about the coming Bridegroom are used to point to our human responsibility to prepare for the King's inevitable return (see Matthew 25).

According to this point of view, the coming kingdom of God promises to bring human history, as we know it, to a close while ushering in a new era of peace, justice, and equity.

Discerning God's Will

Discerning God's Will ■

Discuss the implications of asking in prayer for God to take control of a situation or to decide its outcome. Why do we hesitate to surrender to God in this way? In what ways do you allow God to direct your everyday affairs?

What do you believe happens in God's eternal kingdom that influences what happens in the current reign of God? How do you see your part in this Kingdom? How does knowing you have a part in the Kingdom influence how you think of yourself in relation to God, to others, and to your faith community?

In what ways do your beliefs about the kingdom of God affect the way that you pray about the will of God?

Jewish prayers were not intended to control God; they were designed to ask for God's control and God's will. The surrounding peoples often doubted that their gods had good intentions for them and felt that these gods could be persuaded or controlled somehow by prayers and rituals. By contrast, the Jews believe that God is not capricious, malicious, or neglectful. God acts with a benevolent purpose in human history and is working toward a specific end. Therefore, to pray that God's will be done is an act of submission to God's purpose.

Notice the sentence structure of the petition: "Your kingdom come, / Your will be done" (Matthew 6:10). The kingdom of God and the will of God are inextricably bound together. God's will is revealed as God's kingdom is established. The addition of the phrase "on earth as it is in heaven" reflects the ancient worldview that the cosmos was composed of both earth and heaven. Heaven was a place neither influenced nor controlled by humans where God truly reigns. Just the opposite was believed to be true: What happened in heaven influenced what happened on earth. Earth was a place where humankind consistently resisted God's reign and God's will. At the consummation of God's eternal kingdom, all of earth will come to actualize God's will. In the meantime, Jesus teaches us

Closing Prayer ■

Jesus offered the disciples the Lord's Prayer as a model to teach them how to pray. The first portion of the prayer emphasizes relating to God lovingly as a child adores his or her parent. It also displays the need to approach God with sincere reverence. Last, this prayer establishes priority for God's will and God's kingdom to occur on earth.

At the close of this session, pray the first portion of the Lord's Prayer creatively as a group. Instead of repeating the exact words, pray spontaneously for a deeper, more loving relationship with God and for God's will and kingdom to be expressed through your lives. Invite those who desire to express reverence for God to assume a physical posture of humility while praying.

Preparation for Next Week ■

As a spiritual exercise, make use of the new insights you have learned from this first lesson on the Lord's Prayer. Use the Lord's Prayer as a model to inspire you to pray about your personal relationship with Jesus Christ, your level of reverence toward God, and your willingness to make God's will the first priority of your prayer time.

to pray that we might "emulate" the heavenly state.

As modern-day believers, we continue to struggle to understand Jesus' interpretation of the kingdom of God and the will of God. Though our interpretations may differ, one thing is clear—what we believe about the *kingdom* of God will greatly affect the way we pray about the *will* of God that we hope to see realized "on earth as it is in heaven."

Session Three

Give Us This Day Our Daily Bread

Session Focus ■

This session focuses on the petitions in the Lord's Prayer that concern our need for daily provisions, forgiveness, and protection.

Session Objective ■

The objective of this session is to better understand the kind of human needs that Jesus taught his disciples to address in prayer.

Session Preparation ■

Bring a globe or map of the world and information about where your denomination's missionaries serve. Have several copies of your hymnal on hand and a commentary (such as *The New Interpreter's Bible)* on the Gospel of John. Provide art supplies.

Choose from among these activities and discussion starters to plan your lesson.

Give Us This Day ■

Why do you believe the Lord's Prayer is so widely used throughout Christianity? Which part of the Lord's Prayer is most difficult for contemporary people to understand?

Our Father in heaven,
  hallowed be your name,
  your kingdom come,
  your will be done, on earth as in heaven
Give us today our daily bread.
Forgive us our sins
  as we forgive those who sin against us.
Save us from the time of trial
  and deliver us from evil.
For the kingdom, the power,
  and the glory are yours
  now and for ever. Amen.
(The Lord's Prayer, Ecumenical Text in *The United Methodist Hymnal*, 894; The United Methodist Publishing House, 1989)

Periodically the wording of the Lord's Prayer is updated for modern worshipers. The themes addressed in this prayer remain timeless and are typical of first-century Jewish piety: sanctifying God's name, acknowledging God's rule, requesting forgiveness of sins, and presenting our basic daily needs before a caring and gracious provider. In the previous chapter, we examined the petitions that focus on our relationship with God. In this chapter, we will examine the prayer petitions that address our needs.

Our Daily Bread ■

Name something that you must have on a daily basis. If you were to replace the word *bread* with the item you just named, what word would you use?

In Israel, bread was a major part of the diet. Using a map or globe, locate the country where missionaries are serving or where the church is in mission. What is considered the most important food in the diet there? How is it prepared? How would its absence affect the people who live there?

What is the main food in your country of origin? How is it prepared? How would its absence affect your nutrition?

From this, what do we learn about God's attitude toward our genuine needs?

Look up the passages in Genesis, Luke, and Acts that use bread symbolically. What wider implication do we glean for the understanding of "bread"?

Our Daily Bread

If we look at bulging pantries and freezers stuffed to capacity, we find great difficulty in understanding the importance of this fourth prayer petition. So many people in the Western world have enough food and provisions to last for several days. This is not true, however, for the majority of the world's people. After spending a month with us while we were serving as missionaries in Ghana, West Africa, a close friend made this telling comment: "It seems that a great deal of the day here is spent finding food." She was right! Even in the sparsely populated areas of the city, one could find an outdoor market selling the basic necessities for the evening meal. In the rural areas, women and children often spend the day doing subsistence farming and gathering sticks while the men hunt for enough meat to flavor that night's soup. West Africans are by no means unique; perhaps as many as two-thirds of the world's people spend a great portion of their day gathering or preparing daily provisions.

The people of Jesus' time were not very different. The people of Judea typically ate two meals a day; their Greek and Roman neighbors ate three meals a day. Meat and poultry were generally too expensive to be eaten very often by poor people. Grain, oil, wine, and a limited selection of vegetables and fruits were the diet of the common person. Because of the close proximity of the ocean, the Jordan River, and the Sea of Galilee, fish was an important part of their diet; nevertheless, as much as one-half of the caloric intake of the ancient Mediterranean diet came from bread!

The word *bread* was used symbolically in both Old and New Testament thought and came to mean any kind of food. (See, for example, Genesis 3:19; Luke 15:17; or Acts 2:46.) Thus, a petition for bread, in the context of Jesus' time was extremely significant.

"Bread Theology"

"Bread Theology" ■

If your family miraculously received a box of food every day for a number of years, how might it affect your faith?

The use of the word *daily* must have reminded Jews of their Exodus wanderings, the time when they were forced to depend upon God for daily food. Shortly after their deliverance from slavery in Egypt, centuries before the time of Christ, it became evident that they did not have enough food to complete their journey to the Land of Promise. In response to this basic human need, the children of Israel received a daily miracle. God fed them with manna, a substance like coriander, which appeared from heaven each day for forty years (Exodus 16:14-15, 31-35). The Hebrews used the manna to make their daily bread. Even as they considered this provision against starvation a miracle, they could not resist complaining about it (Numbers 11:1-35).

Israel received daily provisions from God for forty years. How did this affect them? Read Exodus 16:14-15, 31-35 and Numbers 11:4-10. What does this teach us about human nature? How can we guard against taking the blessings of God for granted? In a land where food is in abundance, how should we respond to Jesus' invitation to pray that God provide our daily bread?

Nevertheless, by the end of the Hebrews' wanderings in the wilderness, bread was also equated with God's word (see Deuteronomy 8:3 and Matthew 4:4). Jesus made use of this symbolism when combating Satan in the temptation in the wilderness and when speaking to Jewish dissenters about his divine nature (Matthew 4:1-11 and John 6:30-34).

Some of the Jews of that day were subtly influenced by the surrounding mystery religions like the cults of Isis, Demeter, or Mithras. These mystery religions taught that the spirit was good and that matter, to include the human body, was evil. Therefore, any preoccupation with food for the human body was seen as unspiritual since the body was considered evil. For Jesus to teach his disciples to pray for daily bread was an

The Hebrews did not believe in denigrating the body, which is one reason why *bread* had such a widespread, healthy image. In a culture that worships thinness, what images might you substitute for God's word and for the divine nature of Jesus Christ?

indictment against the notion that the body was inherently evil and should not be cared for.

Bread had its own eschatological significance as well. Prayer for daily bread alluded to the widespread belief that the heavenly manna would reappear in the end times, when all the faithful would feast together in a blessed heavenly banquet with food aplenty for all. Jesus, in John 6:22-59, referred to himself as the "bread of heaven," and "the bread of life," which created yet another controversy among "the Jews." This bread, Jesus said, does not perish in a day nor do those who eat of it. There is a next-life Kingdom dimension to the bread that God provides.

We see then that this simple prayer for daily bread is significant for at least three theological reasons. Primarily, it called for Jewish believers and later for Gentiles to remember the miracle of manna in the wilderness. This miracle spoke of the providential care of God for God's people. Second, a petition for bread stood in opposition to local beliefs that the body was evil and should be punished or deprived. Through this fourth petition of the Lord's Prayer we learn that our basic daily needs are important to God. Third, the prayer acknowledged the eternal promise of a God who would bring justice and bread to all the faithful for eternity in the Kingdom to come.

Forgiveness

For the Jews, forgiveness was a complicated process. Jesus linked sin (or debts) with the petitions on forgiveness. Sin was understood as a huge debt to others and to God, a debt that could not be repaid, as the parable of the unforgiving servant so aptly illustrates (Matthew 18:23-35).

Bible 301 ☐

Have on hand a Bible commentary on the Gospel of John. Read John 6:22-59 and the commentary. What did Jesus mean when he said that he was the bread that came down from heaven? How do you understand the eternal dimension of "bread" for the people of God?

Bible 301 ☐

Look up and sing or read together several of your Communion hymns. How do the lyrics expand the image of "bread" for you? How do they help you understand how Jesus Christ nourishes your body and soul?

Forgiveness ■

Read Matthew 18:23-35 for an understanding of sin as an unpayable debt. If you had to assess your own "indebtedness," what factors would you consider? Either privately or with a partner, journal or discuss how you are similar and dissimilar to the main characters in the parable with regard to debt and willingness to forgive.

In three small groups, look at the three separate passages in Leviticus. How did this ritual of atonement work? Though it might seem like an antiquated and ineffectual practice, consider the idea of sacrifice in the context of repentance and forgiveness. Do this through the "back door"—take turns recalling a superficial apology or request for forgiveness (unless to do so would reopen wounds that you are not equipped to care for in this setting). For example, "I'm sorry you feel that way" really isn't an apology; it shows no repentance, and it requires nothing of the one who offers it.

What is an appropriate "sacrifice," if we're fresh out of goats, in a sincere request for forgiveness to someone whom we have wronged? What kind of sacrifice, if any, does God request of us? If a petition for forgiveness is not offered as a prayer to God also, is anything lacking? If so, what more might be needed? How does understanding any request for forgiveness of another as a prayer to God at the same time change your thinking about forgiveness? about prayer?

How does one even begin to make amends to God? The levitical system of offerings and sacrifices offered several ways for the Jews to restore breaches in their relationship with God. Yom Kippur, or the Day of Atonement, instituted in Leviticus 16, was a yearly fast day, observed for the purpose of removing sin from *all* individuals in Israel. On the Day of Atonement, the people confessed sin and prayed for forgiveness for the entire congregation of Israel. Two goats were used sacrificially. The first goat was a sin offering that cleansed all the portions of their worship space (sanctuary, tent of meeting, altar) from any human sin that had penetrated into any of these sacred areas. The priest confessed the sins of the nation over the second goat, the scapegoat, who was then released into the wilderness—symbolically carrying the sins of the nation along with it.

Individual offenses against God were handled differently. According to the law, some offenses were unforgivable and merited the death penalty. For other offenses, individuals were allowed to offer sacrifices like the guilt offering (Leviticus 5:15-16) or the sin offering (Leviticus 5:1-6) to expiate, or make redress for, their offenses.

Forgiveness between peers was also complicated and involved more than exchanging words of forgiveness. Before a person could be forgiven, by Jewish custom, he or she must first have demonstrated repentance. Five basic steps were involved in repentance: (1) recognizing sin; (2) remorse; (3) turning away from the sin; (4) restitution where possible; and (5) confession. By the provisions of Jewish law, the offended person could reserve the right to receive some form of restitution from the person who had offended him or her. The person who committed the offense

Examine and discuss the steps of *teshuva*. In your own culture, list the steps necessary to receive forgiveness from another person. Is an attempt at restitution expected before receiving forgiveness in your culture? Explain. How do you know when you need to ask God for forgiveness? Is it difficult for you to pray for forgiveness? How do you know if God has forgiven you? When our relationship with God is not good, does God require us to *do* something to restore that relationship? If so, what?

How do you know if a person has really forgiven you? How do you know if you have really forgiven someone who has wronged you? What responsibility, if any, does the offended person have to work toward reconciliation?

was expected to make some attempt at this restitution. Jewish scholar David Blumenthal, in explaining the stages and steps of *teshuva* (repentance), points out, "When one sins against another, one incurs an obligation to right the wrong one has committed. . . . The more serious the wrong, the more serious the obligation to set it straight ("Repentance and Forgiveness," *Cross Currents*, Spring 1998).

Once these conditions had been met, the person who had been offended was bound morally, though not legally, to forgive the offender. The most basic kind of forgiveness was to relinquish one's claim for restitution against the offender. Note that this forgiveness did not require an emotional investment in becoming reconciled with or empathetic with the offender.

A second kind of forgiveness was an act of the heart. It involved empathy with the plight of the offender. Jesus' parable about the unforgiving servant in Matthew 18:23-35 models this kind of forgiveness that goes beyond the demands of the law and reaches into the realm of relationships. It was in this religious context that Jesus instructed his disciples to pray, "Forgive us our sins as we forgive those who sin against us."

Deliverance

Deliverance

The ecumenical text of the Lord's Prayer substitutes the words: *"Save us from the time of trial"* for *"Lead us not into temptation."* What new insights does this alternate reading provide for you?

At first glance, a prayer for God to refrain from leading us into situations where we would be tempted seems contradictory to all we know about the nature and the will of God. In actuality, this is more of a translation problem than a theological problem. The Greek word, *peirasmon*, historically rendered "temptation" in Matthew 6:13, could also be rendered "trial" or "test." In the English language, the word *temptation* carries negative connotations; but a trial or a test can easily be viewed as a learning experience. A more accurate rendering of this petition can be found in the Ecumenical Text of the Lord's Prayer: "Save us from the time of trial."

Examine the biblical texts about testing. What do you think is the difference between being tested and having to deal with the delays and frustrations of daily life? Does God test us? If not, what is the place of the tests we have to face in life? If they are not of God, what are they?

Jews believed that God tested them. See, for example, Abraham's testing in Genesis 22:1-2, or Jesus' testing in what we commonly call the Temptation (Matthew 4:1). Situations like these were accepted and perhaps almost expected aspects of life.

In addition, Jesus taught his disciples that a time of hard testing would come before his Second Coming. This period of time is sometimes called the *Parousia* (see Matthew 24). Many believe that this prayer petition to be spared hard testing refers to a time of trial (or tribulation) preceding the second coming of Christ.

Does the anticipation of Christ's second coming affect how you pray? If so, how?

Though the human family does not always agree about the origin or the nature of evil, the *problem* of evil remains a frequent topic of discussion in most cultures. How do we, as human beings, deal with the suffering and devastation that evil metes out to us?

What Kind of Evil?

What Kind of Evil?

Why do you think Jesus found it necessary to include a specific request concerning evil in the Lord's Prayer? Is it still relevant to pray that we be delivered from evil? If so, why?

The Greek word used for "evil" in this passage could mean either "evil things" or "the evil one." Both uses are found elsewhere in the New Testament. This is, perhaps, more of a problem for us than it was for Jesus' followers.

Our modern theologians typically classify evil in two categories: moral and natural (or physical). Moral evil is usually ascribed to human agents whose intent is to harm. Examples would include murder, theft, and lying. Natural evil typically refers to natural or physical events that are considered evil

When we pray the Lord's Prayer, are we praying to be delivered from evil things or from an evil personality?

Not all persons believe that there is a separate entity or phenomenon of evil, but that some degree of wrong or willfulness resides in each human spirit that operates contrary to the will of God. How do you sort out the presence and manifestation of evil? Where do you think evil comes from?

The biblical community often held that evil or sin was at the root of events like serious illnesses or unpredictable misfortunes. What place, if any, does evil play in these events now?

Distribute art supplies of various kinds and create some rendering of "evil." Is there a tempter? If so, is the tempter inherently evil? Do you think there is a place for temptation in God's plan for humankind? If so, how would you describe it? How does praying to be delivered from temptation strengthen your faith and enhance your life?

because of the harm they cause. Examples include earthquakes, droughts, disease, and death.

If we assume that the evil spoken of in the Lord's Prayer refers exclusively to *evil things*, any local newspaper would provide us numerous reasons to pray for deliverance from evil. When thinking about the existence of moral evil, our modern minds tend to ask questions like *what* in the environment or the society caused a person to commit evil deeds? When investigating the reasons for natural evils, we often look for environmental factors that we can neither predict nor control.

As modern Christians, we are more than eager to pray that God would rescue us from *evil things*. We are sometimes, however, less comfortable with praying for deliverance from the *evil one*. If, somehow, Jesus' contemporaries were able to read our newspapers, they would add another element of causality to their interpretation of both the natural and moral evils that surround us. They would ask, *Who* caused those people to be morally evil? *Who* caused those natural disasters that harmed good as well as evil people? For many of the Jews of Jesus' day, the answer would be the evil one.

Jesus paired the two petitions about forgiveness and deliverance from trial. Because we mortals are weak, we will constantly find ourselves faltering and being on both the giving and receiving ends of evil. For this reason we pray that we not be dragged into transgression by the evil one or by evil circumstances and that we be forgiven when we perpetrate the evil. Jesus is our advocate against the evil one; he also acquits us before God, provided that we have heeded the petition to forgive others, as the two verses that are

How much do our beliefs about angels and evil entities influence our prayers today? How do the various cultural media feed or inform our beliefs?

Bible 301 ☐

Read the passages about Satan and his control in the world, and read through Tobit, if your Bible has an Apocrypha. Form pairs and imagine that one of you is from another country, visiting the United States. After spending a month watching television, going to the movies, and reading the most popular books, have a conversation about the belief in and the presence of evil things or the evil one. What new insights surface? Did your religious beliefs influence in any way the media's portrayals? If so, how?

Where Is the Last Part? ◼

How are doxologies used in your congregation's worship? Do you ever find yourself unconsciously humming the tune or singing the words to the songs that your church uses in worship? Have you thought of this as another form of prayer?

often ignored at the end of the prayer confirm (Matthew 6:14-15). The evil one would have us believe that we are not forgiven and that he is in control of the world (4:8-9).

During the period of time between the Old and New Testaments, elaborate systems of belief developed concerning the activities of both angels and demons (fallen angels). The Intertestamental books of Tobit and First Enoch illustrate how this emerging emphasis upon the supernatural affected the Jews of that time. By New Testament times, it was commonly believed that Satan had control over the world (Luke 4:6; John 12:31; 14:30) and could trouble its inhabitants. Satan's whims and wishes would be carried out by lesser supernatural personalities, known as devils or demons. Many of the Jews believed that these personalities influenced both people and the elements and were frequently the cause of disease (Matthew 4:24; 12:22-24). Certain Jews practiced rites of exorcism. Yet, Scripture also notes that the Sadducees did not believe in angels, demons, or spirits (Acts 23:8). In such an environment, it was highly relevant that prayer address the problem of evil.

Where Is the Last Part of the Prayer?

The oldest and most reliable Greek texts of the New Testament do not include the final portion of the Lord's Prayer that we typically say: "For the kingdom, the power, and the glory are yours now and forever." Therefore, modern Bible translations, such as the New International Version or the New Revised Standard Version, do not include it in the formal text of Matthew 6:13. The last sentence is thought to be a doxology that Christians later added because it had become accepted as part of the prayer.

A *doxology* is an expression of praise to God. Perhaps one of the most popular doxologies of our times is

Bible 301 ☐

Look in your hymnal index for doxologies and for stanzas of hymns that are doxological. How do they summarize and affirm the power of God in our lives?

Praise God, from whom all blessings flow;
praise him, all creatures here below;
praise him above, ye heavenly host;
praise Father, Son, and Holy Ghost. Amen.

Scholars generally believe that doxologies were used in Israel's worship at the end of hymns or prayers. The New Testament church retained many elements of Jewish worship including the use of doxologies. They were used frequently in the writings of Paul (see Galatians 1:5; 1 Timothy 1:17; or 2 Corinthians 1:3-4) and in worship. The concluding words of the Lord's Prayer are similar to one of David's doxologies found in 1 Chronicles 29:11, which speaks of the kingdom, power, and glory of God.

Summary

As you conclude today's lesson, review the principles of prayer learned both in this week and last week's lessons:

- God wants to be considered as close to us as a trusted parent.
- While we consider God as accessible as a human parent, we yet acknowledge the "otherness" of God. Nothing about God is common or ordinary, not even God's name.
- We acknowledge God as our Ruler and pray that God's kingdom and God's will prevail—even over our own.
- God is the One to whom we look for all our daily needs, and those needs are important to God.
- In order to maintain a vital relationship

with God, we must walk in forgiveness with one another and seek forgiveness from God.

- Through the petition concerning temptation and evil, we learn that God is concerned about the things that try us and the evils that surround us. God is our Protector and Defender.
- Finally, the early church had become so accustomed to closing the Lord's Prayer with words of praise that they added familiar words of praise to the end of the prayer.

Closing Prayer ■

Oh, God, you are as close to us as a trusted family member, while at the same time being so holy that we whisper your name. Help us to become comfortable in your awesome presence. Teach us to recognize what you want for this world so that we might pray for your will and your Kingdom to be revealed. Remember our daily needs, both temporal and spiritual. Teach us how to love and forgive one another. Protect us, even from forces we do not understand. Let even the lives we lead bring you praise, for all praise belongs to you. Amen.

Close with one of the doxologies you identified earlier.

Preparation for Next Week ■

As a spiritual exercise, write several short prayers based on the themes to which you normally give the least attention. (Consider continuing this exercise during the week as a means of reprioritizing your prayer requests.)

Session Four

Prayer Parables

Session Focus

In this session, we will examine the prayers that other people prayed in Jesus' time by looking at imprecatory prayers and prayer parables.

Session Objective

The objective of this session is to encourage the participants to discover what motivates him or her to pray as we look at the topics of prayer and vengeance, prayer and the deceased, prayer and persistence, and prayer and self-righteousness.

Session Preparation

Have on hand a Bible dictionary.

Choose from among these activities and discussion starters to plan your lesson.

Prayer Against Enemies?

The disciples had Jesus as their teacher; yet, they still needed more instruction in prayer. Reflect on your spiritual journey. Who are your "prayer mentors"?

Of the four Gospels, it is said that Luke's Gospel contains the most teachings about prayer. Luke told his story in two books of the New Testament, Luke and Acts, in the form of letters written to a friend named Theophilus. The Book of Luke is organized around four major themes: genealogy and birth (Luke 1–4:13), the Galilean ministry (Luke 4:14–9:50), the journey to Jerusalem (Luke 9:51–19:44), and the arrest and Crucifixion (Luke 19:45–24:53). In this chapter, we will explore one of the disciples' would-be prayers and three of the prayer parables found in Luke's travel account.

Prayer Against Our Enemies?

In spite of Jesus' repeated efforts to teach his disciples how to pray by word and by example, they still needed more instruction in prayer. When the people of a Samaritan village rejected Jesus, the disciples wanted to curse them by calling down fire to destroy their village (Luke 9:51-56). This incident opens our discussion of prayer and cursing.

Luke 9:51 marks the beginning of what is known as Luke's travel narratives. Jesus was on a mission that would culminate with his own death in Jerusalem. As the days approached, Jesus set his face toward Jerusalem. *Set his face* is an Old Testament idiom used also in Ezekiel (see Ezekiel 20:46; 21:2; 25:2) that conveys determination and purpose.

To what methods of spiritual instruction do you best respond? Name several important lessons about prayer that you have learned through life's experiences.

Bible 301 ☐

Look up Samaria *and* Samaritan *in a Bible dictionary. What were the main points of conflict and contention between the Jews and the Samaritans?*

Read John 4 and Luke 9:51-56 for two instances of Jesus' encounter with Samaritans. What happened in each of those instances? How did Jesus, the disciples, and the Samaritans receive and treat each other? Why do you think Jesus went through Samaria with the disciples despite the obvious tensions between Jews and Samaritans?

Examine the practice of imprecatory prayers. Read the Scripture examples in Second Kings and Psalms. Under what conditions, if any, would it be acceptable to pray *imprecatory* prayers (prayers against someone else)? Some persons who feel they act in faith also feel that

Jesus' journey took him through Samaria, which was highly unusual. Tensions were so great between the Jews and the Samaritans that Jewish travelers usually walked miles out of their way to avoid coming into contact with the Samaritans.

Jesus did not avoid the Samaritans; he had walked through Samaria many times before. In Jesus' lengthy discourse with the Samaritan woman in John 4, we learn that the place of worship was one of the points of disagreement between the Jews and the Samaritans. For a number of historical reasons, the Samaritans worshiped on Mt. Gerizim, while the Jews insisted that Jerusalem was the place that God had designated for worship and sacrifice. It is presumed that some Samaritans were offended to hear that Jesus was on his way to Jerusalem and thus refused him hospitality as he was passing through. Their rejection, in turn, offended the disciples who asked permission to call fire down from heaven to consume them!

Where did the disciples get such an idea? In the context of the Old Testament, their request was not as unusual as it appears to us. Prayers of cursing or *imprecatory* prayers, were part of the Old Testament canon. It was widely known that the Old Testament prophet Elijah had called fire down to consume his enemies (2 Kings 1:10). Several psalms, some of which were used in worship, contained curses against the king's enemies (see, for example, Psalm 59 and Psalm 109). The disciples were acquainted with the concept of cursing one's enemies and considered it an acceptable practice. This raises a critical question for us today: Is it ever acceptable to curse our enemies in prayer?

For an answer, look at Jesus' response to

their enemies are therefore God's enemies. How do you assess this belief?

Were the disciples justified in feeling offended by the Samaritans' apparent lack of hospitality? If so, why did Jesus stop them from cursing the Samaritans by calling fire down upon them? (Luke 9:55). How should the disciples have responded to the Samaritans?

Can you identify groups of people that you either consciously or unconsciously avoid? How might the lack of interaction with "contemporary Samaritans" affect the content and focus of our prayers?

Read the Scriptures in this section on blessing and cursing one's enemies. How would Jesus, Paul, James, and Peter advise us to relate to our enemies? How challenging is this for you to do? In all of the passages cited in this section, what are the motives for action? List them and add to the list throughout the session.

The Rich Man and Lazarus ■

Read Luke 16:19-31. Quickly jot down the main points in these categories: the characters (social status, personal traits), where

the disciples. Most modern translations simply report that he turned and rebuked them (Luke 9:55). Based on some ancient manuscripts, some older translations, like the King James Version, add: "Ye know not what manner of spirit ye are of. For the Son of Man is not come to destroy men's lives, but to save them." This extra explanation, which may have been added by the early church, is not inconsistent with the rebuke.

How, then, should we treat our enemies? In the Sermon on the Mount, Jesus encourages us to do good to our enemies, love those who hate us and bless the very ones who curse us (Matthew 5:43-46; Luke 6:27-28). Jesus became an example of this principle in Luke 23:34 when he refused to curse even those who were crucifying him and instead prayed for them.

Though the apostle Paul did curse his enemies in Galatians 1:9, he echoes Jesus' teaching on the subject in Romans 12:14 when he exhorts his readers to bless and not curse. James, in his discussion on the evils of the tongue, points to the inconsistency of blessings and cursing coming from the same person (James 3:8-10). Peter encourages his audience to resist returning evil for evil (1 Peter 3:9) and to imitate, instead, the example of Christ who refused to return insults (1 Peter 2:23). Clearly, the New Testament teaches a new ideal, which is to pray for the redemption rather than punishment of our enemies.

The Rich Man and Lazarus

This parable (Luke 16:19-31) revolves around the fictitious story of an unnamed rich man and a beggar who sat at his gate. On one of many reversals, the poor man is named; *Lazarus* means "God is my help."

the action takes place, reversals of circumstance, who interacts with whom and with what result.

Form two teams. Team One will be part of Father Abraham's, "review board," charged with evaluating Divas's petition. Team Two will be Divas's brothers. First, the review board will consider whether to inter-cede with the brothers and why. (Instruct them that they can do so if they want to). Based on that deci-sion, Team Two will work out an ending to the para-ble that shows what hap-pens to the brothers.

What difference can inter-cession make in life? If you could know in advance what effect your interces-sion for another might make, might that prompt you to pray or to act differ-ently? If so, how? What spiritual lessons does this parable have for you?

(The rich man has traditionally been called "Divas," though this is not a name but a translation from the Latin adjective meaning "rich." In the story, we gain little informa-tion about either of the main characters except for their economic condition.

The rich man was scandalously wealthy. He wore the finest clothes available to him. The purple clothing he wore was believed to have been dyed with a rare dye made from shellfish; and the linen was thought to be an Egyptian linen, often called woven air, made into highly sought-after undergarments. He feasted every day in a land where the com-mon people ate a monotonous and often meatless diet.

Lazarus was extremely poor as well as sick, being covered with sores. He lay at the gate of the rich man's house and longed to have the crumbs that fell or were dropped from the rich man's table. These "crumbs" would have been hunks of bread that the rich were in the habit of using to wipe their hands in the absence of napkins. These huge bread crumbs are believed to be those referred to in the story of the Syrophonecian woman when she said that even the dogs were allowed to eat the crumbs that fell from the table (Matthew 15:27). In Lazarus' case, not only did he not get what would have served as dog food, even the dogs licked at him.

When the rich man died, he was buried, presumably with all the pomp and honor that befitted his station in life. The Bible tells us that the angels attended to the death of the poor man, carrying him to the "bosom" of Abraham (KJV, RSV), which could be seen as the equivalent of heaven. It is here that Jesus' story takes an unexpected turn. While poor Lazarus is in heaven, the wealthy man found himself being tormented in the place that

The Jews believed that prosperity came to the deserving and poverty came as punishment. In the United States, some believe that success (or blessing) comes to people who pull themselves up by their bootstraps. How might "bootstraps theology" influence our attitude toward the poor in our society?

In this parable, the lifestyle of the rich man appears to have affected the way he related to poor people. What does the conventional wisdom of our society say about the reasons for poverty and our corporate responsibility for the poor? How does this affect the way we treat the poor?

Review the Scriptures about "tormenting fire." Is this a threat we take seriously today? If we did, what effect might it have on our prayer life and daily behavior? What effect might the absence of human suffering have on our prayer life?

English Bibles frequently translate "hell." We are never really told why he was there, but his presence is intended to send a warning.

The parable of the rich man and Lazarus addresses several critical issues involving the afterlife. The Jews at that time believed that prosperity and abundance were gifts from God and that poverty came to the slothful and the disobedient. Jesus, in this parable, makes a clear statement that riches are no indicator of either character or favor with God. The parable should not, however, be considered a blanket indictment against all rich people, for Abraham, who received Lazarus in "heaven," was a very wealthy man in his day.

It is also important to note that the Jewish belief of Jesus' time had unclear notions about what happened to people when they died. Some believed that the dead slept in the underworld in a place called Sheol, which English versions of the Old Testament alternate between translating as "hell" or "the grave." Others believed that there was a place where both good and bad had a foretaste of eternal reward or punishment. Some of these beliefs emerged in the Intertestamental period and can be documented in the literature of that time, known as the Apocrypha and Pseudepigrapha.

In this parable, Jesus validates belief in a place of punishment with tormenting fire (see also Matthew 5:22; 18:9; Mark 9:43, for example) and a contrasting place of peace, Abraham's bosom. Neither the rich man nor Lazarus is sleeping in his grave; they are both aware of their surroundings. The afterlife is not a place for conversion or to correct mistakes. We find the rich man behaving just as he did on earth, inclined to order Lazarus around as he once did his servants (Luke 16:24). In spite of his petitions, the rich man's fate is sealed; not even father Abraham is inclined help him in the smallest way (16:25-26). Nor will Abraham take a warning message to his unsuspecting siblings. The message is clear here: The remaining family members have ample evidence and instruction in the law; if they choose not to attend to their duty and the obligations of their faith, Abraham will not force them to do so.

Prayer to ■
the Saints

This parable also explores the role that prayer plays in the afterlife. After a person is dead, is it too late to pray for him or her? Why or why not?

The rich man wanted Abraham to send Lazarus back to warn his brothers. What role do you feel departed saints are able to play in our earthly affairs today? What message does Jesus' parable convey about prayer and the dead?

What do you think about the early church's notion of both praying for deceased saints and needing their prayers? about the role of Jesus Christ as our only intercessor?

Prayer to the Saints

This passage raises the issue of prayer to the saints. It seems that the practice of praying to the saints began with the early church's practice of praying *for* them after their death. Initially, any Christian who died was remembered in prayer in services that were held on the third, seventh, ninth, thirteenth, and fortieth days after their death. Over time, the church began to draw up lists of martyrs, believing that prayer was "of great benefit to those for whom it is offered" (Cyril of Jerusalem). Even Origen, a well-known early church father, said that praying for the saints attested to the unity of Christians in heaven and on earth. He also noted that prayer should be offered only to God through Christ, though prayers directly to Jesus Christ have been heaven-sent for centuries. Before long, other leaders in the church began to teach that *we* needed the prayers of the saints more than *they* needed ours, saying: "Only God can pardon, though we see the merits of the martyrs have great weight before his tribunal" (Cyprian of Carthage). Typically, Protestants follow the words of Jesus to pray in his name, and do not pray to the saints.

The Bible teaches us that we have only

What do you think were the motivations for all of the characters in this parable-drama? Add them to the list.

Read Romans 8:34; 1 John 2:1; and Hebrews 7:25. What do these Scripture passages teach us about Jesus' role in prayer?

The Woman and the Unjust Judge ▪

The widow and the judge in this parable are symbols of the weak and the powerful in their culture. Read Luke 18:1-8. What contemporary positions of power parallel that of the unjust judge? What message does this parable convey to people who sit in positions of power today?

What group of people in our contemporary society would you compare to the widow in today's parable? What hope does this parable offer to people today who feel powerless?

one mediator in prayer, Jesus Christ (1 Timothy 2:5) who is seated in the place of authority and continues to make intercession for us (Romans 8:34; 1 John 2:1; Hebrews 7:25). Nor are we left to our own devices; when we do not know how to pray, the Holy Spirit intercedes for us (Romans 8:26-27).

Turning again to the parable of the rich man and Lazarus, we learn several important lessons: (1) We cannot judge a person by his or her station in life. (2) There is life after death. (3) The choices we make in life are the determining factors that influence what happens to us after death. (4) Even though we pray directly to God or through Christ or through the most venerable of saints, like Father Abraham, prayer requests must be in the will of God.

The Woman and the Unjust Judge

In the parable of the widow and the unjust judge (Luke 18:1-8), we are reminded that Jesus often taught as the rabbis by making frequent use of comparisons and contrasts. Note the contrasts between the woman and this judge.

The judge sat in position of power. The fact that he was called a *judge* and not a member of the Sanhedrin *Council* suggests that he was one of the Roman magistrates. He ruled at a time when justice could easily be redirected for a bribe. It was commonly said that these judges could be bought for a dish of meat. The passage itself tells us that he had no respect for either people or God (Luke 18:2).

The widow, by contrast, was considered one of the weakest members of her society. The Old Testament was filled with requirements to care for the widows and the orphans. By society's dictates, women were dependent upon men all their lives: their fathers until marriage, their husbands once married, and their eldest sons if widowed. Women in Jesus' time had very few rights. Even their capacity to inherit property was open to dispute. One of the ironies in this passage is that this widow repeatedly insisted that the judge do his duty to her under the law.

The only thing the parable tells us about this woman is that she kept appearing before this judge with the same petition: "Grant me justice against my opponent" (Luke 18:3). It would appear from the scanty information that we have received that this woman was motivated by her hunger for justice. That judge, no matter how dishonest he might have been, symbolized justice. The woman, in spite of being assigned one of the lowest positions of power in her culture, never stopped believing in the principle of justice; and eventually she received it. For this kind of faith, Jesus applauded the widow. If this scene had taken place in our times, would we label the widow's persistence as stubbornness, will power, or faith?

The Bible offers us so many prayer promises (Matthew 21:22; Mark 11:24; John 15:7; and so forth), yet many of us live under the pall of unanswered prayer. There are several encouraging lessons we can learn from this parable of the widow and the judge.

First, delays are not denials. For a variety of reasons, there will be delays in receiving an answer to some of our prayers; yet, Jesus applauds those who continue faithfully in prayer. This parable is often taught alongside the parable of the persistent friend, which contains the familiar encouragement to keep on asking, keep on seeking, and keep on

What is the place of justice in this parable? in intercession and petition? If this scene had taken place in our society, would we call the widow's persistence willpower or faith? Why?

Read these Scriptures about prayer promises. Do you think there is such a thing as unanswered prayer? How do you interpret the perceived absence of an answer in prayer? What do you do if your prayer remains unanswered for a long period of time?

The parable demonstrates the importance of persistence in prayer. What inspired the woman to continue making what appeared to be a futile request? What inspires you to continue to pray when things look hopeless?

What, if anything, is the difference between persistence and stubbornness in prayer? How do we know when to stop praying about a situation?

What do you think are proper motivators in prayer? (Add them to the list.) How does the judge help illuminate the justice we can expect from God?

Read the passages from John about praying in Jesus' name. What does it mean to pray in Jesus' name? How do you discern what is in the interests of the Kingdom?

At heart, the parable is about faithfulness. How does it illustrate the faithfulness of God for you and the call to our own faithfulness in prayer and discernment of God's will? What is the good news in this parable for us?

knocking (Luke 11:5-13), until we receive what we need from God.

Second, through Jesus' favorable reaction to the widow's persistence in prayer, we infer that more than merely the hope of personal gain motivated the woman to continue her crusade. In her case, a principle was involved—justice. Somewhere in the process of appearing and reappearing before the judge, the widow must have decided that she would rather endure humiliation than forego any hope of justice. She was also a constant reminder to the judge that the law obligated him to care for the orphan and widow.

Third, why do we tenaciously cling to a prayer request? Who stands to gain from an answer to our prayers? For whose kingdom and glory are we praying? In prayer, the difference between willpower and faith is found in motive. In John 14:13 and John 16:23, Jesus promised to answer prayers that were prayed in his name. To pray in Jesus' name means to pray as Jesus would have prayed, for the best interests of the kingdom of God. As a missionary, I learned that God was much more likely to be concerned about our need for transportation to get God's work done than about our preferences in the color or model of a car. An understanding of the difference between our own personal motives and the needs of the kingdom of God will often help us determine when and how to persist in prayer.

Perhaps most importantly, we see here both the promise of God's faithfulness to us and the call to our own faithfulness to God. In many parables, the main character is a God-figure. In this case, the judge stands in contrast to God. If the judge, who does not regard God or persons, can be moved to do the right thing for a nearly helpless citizen in his jurisdiction, how much more so will God tend to the needs of those for whom God has promised to care. Likewise, if the widow, whose voice was among the most disregarded and marginal in her society, could persist in her petition for rightful protection, any and all of God's children can come to God with expectation and hope as God wishes.

The Pharisee and the Tax Collector

The Jews held a belief that God was especially attentive to prayers offered in the Temple (see 1 Kings 8:27-30), thus many people made an effort to be in the Temple courts at the hour of prayer. The hours of prayer observed by the devout were 9 A.M., noon, and 3 P.M. Those who were unable to go to the Temple often prayed facing the direction of the Temple. It was at such a sacred hour of prayer that the Pharisee and the tax collector were both found praying in the Temple (Luke 18:9-14).

The Pharisees of that time often gauged righteousness by how rigidly a person observed the law. (Their conflicts with Jesus were usually about how well he upheld their particular standards, even though he acted within the bounds of the law.) This particular Pharisee, in a manner characteristic of his sect, came to prayer to inform God of how he had exceeded the demands of the law in both fasting and tithing (verse 12).

Jews were obliged to fast only on the Day of Atonement. Some Pharisees, however, also fasted two days of each week, days that just happened to coincide with market days in Jerusalem. To insure that more people would be aware of their piety, they often whitened their faces and made themselves appear weak. Jesus indirectly condemned their actions in the Sermon on the Mount, when

The Pharisee and the Tax Collector

The Jews believed that God was especially attentive to prayers offered at the Temple, which they did at several fixed times. Where do you believe that God is most likely to hear your prayers? What times of day have you found best for personal prayer?

Read Matthew 6:16-18. Why did Jesus encourage his followers to fast in private? Do you or members of your church practice fasting as a spiritual discipline? When we fast, we usually deny ourselves food, comfort, or pleasure. What role does self-denial play in prayer? How often should we fast?

With a partner or privately in your journal, reflect on how the combination of prayer with other spiritual disciplines (such as fasting, reading Scripture, engaging in acts of hospitality, or other disciplines) have enhanced your spiritual sensitivities. Have you seen your spiritual life grow through these practices? How might your experience help another Christian grow?

Read or act out Luke 18:9-
14. The Pharisee in this
parable appeared obliged
to inform God that in fasting and tithing he had
exceeded the demands of
the law. Why do you think
he felt the need to
"impress" God?

Do you find it easier to
pray or to do righteous
deeds? When we perform
acts of righteousness (or do
good deeds), do these good
deeds make us more right-
eous in God's sight? Why or
why not?

The tax collector seemed to
do everything wrong, yet
Jesus spoke well of his
prayers. Why? Does this
mean that it does not matter if we continue to sin as
long as we are sincere
when we do pray? Give reasons for your response.

From the context of this
parable, compare and con-
trast the spiritual lives of
the Pharisee and the tax
collector. Why did each
man come to the Temple
that day? Where did each
man stand? What physical
posture did each man
assume? On what basis did
each of them approach
God in prayer? From what
you know of the general
character of the Pharisees
and of tax collectors, how
would you have "rated"
their prayers?

What were the motivations
for each man's prayers?
(Add them to the list.)

he instructed the disciples to avoid looking
dismal when they fasted (Matthew 6:16-18)
in order to impress others.

The laws of tithing required that persons
give a tenth of their increase each year to the
Levites, who were the designated priests of
Israel. There were certain items exempt from
this tithe. The Pharisees tithed from everything they owned, including the exempt
herbs and spices used for cooking, hoping to
court greater favor with God and the people
(see Luke 11:42).

Tax collectors were generally considered
sinners (Matthew 9:10; 11:19; Luke 15:1).
They were Jews who collected taxes from
their fellow citizens for an oppressive foreign
government—the Romans. In addition to
this insult, they usually added fraudulently to
the tax bill and pocketed the difference.
From his brief prayer, it does not appear that
the tax collector was planning to abandon his
occupation. To do so would have been quite
costly. As indicated in a previous chapter, one
of the prerequisites to being forgiven was an
attempt on the part of the sinner at making
restitution. According to the law of Moses
this tax collector would have been obligated
to restore fourfold all that he had fraudulently received from the taxpayers (Exodus 22:1).
Undoubtedly, with the weight of his distance
from God's grace in mind, the tax collector
stood at a distance and beat his breast in
contrition while he prayed for God's mercy.

The key to understanding this parable can
be found in its first verse. The parable was
directed to those who trusted in their own
righteousness and regarded others with con-
tempt (Luke 18:9). Compare the Pharisee's
prayer to the Lord's Prayer. The Pharisee in
no way honored God's name or exalted
God's kingdom. There is no mention made

Spend a few minutes with two or three other persons thinking about a discernment process for listening to God through prayer, fasting, or other spiritual practice. What ways have been helpful, even transformational, in allowing you to discern God's will for you? Take time to pray with these partners for God's guidance; then pray the closing prayer with the whole group.

Closing Prayer ■

Gracious God, the prayers of the disciples and the parables concerning prayer reveal that we are still confused about our own prayers. We vacillate between the mean-spirited vindictiveness of the disciples and the admirable persistence of the widow. Like the Pharisee, we dare to appear before you with a laundry list of our spiritual achievements. Teach us to trust in your goodness and not in our feeble acts of righteousness when we pray. We ask these things in Jesus' name. Amen.

Preparation for Next Week ■

In today's lesson, you have examined and listed the motives involved in imprecatory prayers, prayer to the saints, persistence in prayer, and self-righteous prayers. During this coming week, examine your own prayer motives. Why do you pray as you do?

of his relationship with God or of his dependence upon God. Instead, the Pharisee boldly stood in the Temple and gave his status report: *I thank you that I am better than others. . . . These are the wonderful things that I do. . . .*

By contrast, the tax collector was painfully aware that he was far from God's standard of righteousness. He had no deeds in which to take his refuge; we hear of nothing in his prayer about any good he had done. His only refuge was in the mercy of God. The tax collector did not leave the Temple justified because he was the more righteous. He was justified because he understood that God is the *source* of righteousness.

Prayer and Healing

Session Focus ■

The focus of this chapter is healing: its significance in the New Testament world, its symbolism, and the circumstances surrounding how several New Testament persons received their healing.

Session Objective ■

Our objective will be to better understand the roles that faith, intercession, symbolism, and our relationship with God play in healing.

Session Preparation ■

Look at your book of worship or hymnal to see if it contains healing services and prayers. Have on hand a Bible commentary, a Bible dictionary, and hymnals or a book of worship.

Choose from among these activities and discussion starters to plan your lesson.

Blind Bartimaeus ■

Bartimaeus knew that Jesus was near because of the crowds that surrounded him. How do *we* know when God is present?

Bartimaeus may have been a street beggar, but he knew

This chapter stands in strong contrast to the previous chapters in which we examined the prayers of Jesus and others. Here, we will explore some of the *conversations* that Jesus had with people in the process of their healing, which we may think about as *prayers*. Then, we will look at the prayer that Jesus prayed before raising Lazarus from death.

Blind Bartimaeus

Near the end of his ministry, Jesus healed a blind man who lived near Jericho (Mark 10:46-52). Matthew (20:29-34) and Luke (18:35-43) also told this story with a few variations, but only Mark tells us the man's name. Bartimaeus, literally "the son of Timaeus," was begging by the roadside when he heard from the crowd that Jesus was there. Suddenly, he began to shout: "Jesus, Son of David, have mercy on me!" (Mark 10:47).

Bartimaeus's Acclamation

No messianic attribution has been used in Mark's Gospel to this point. However, as Mark's narrative brings Jesus to the brink of his Passion, Mark has introduced the messianic title as a foretaste of the Davidic images his readers will encounter in the coming account of the Crucifixion and Resurrection.

about his Jewish faith and tradition. What assumptions do we normally make about the faith of beggars and street people? How do most Christian communities respond when beggars and street people come to their places of worship to pray? What does your own faith community do?

Son of David ■

Form five small groups. Divide these Scriptures among them: Isaiah 11:1-12; 35:5-6; 42:6-7; 61:1-2; Jeremiah 33:14-16. What do they say about the coming of the Son of David? about the Kingdom this Son would inaugurate?

Bible 301 ☐

Using a concordance and a Bible dictionary, look up the terms Son of David *and* messiah. *How are they related? What does the Son of David / Messiah mean for the Jews? Why do you think Bartimaeus's use of the title* Son of David *was so important to Jesus? Why would a blind man have been so interested in the Son of David?*

Some, surprised by the sudden outburst from a blind beggar, may have turned around to see what was happening. There were others in the crowd, however, who were annoyed by his boldness and told him to be quiet (10:48). Bartimaeus, who was familiar with rejection, ignored them and shouted all the more: "Son of David, have mercy on me!"

Son of David

In the midst of his insistent salutation, Mark has the blind man reveal a theological truth: Jesus as the Messiah. Why was this so important? "Son of David" is a messianic title. The prophets foretold that the Messiah would come from the lineage of David (Isaiah 11:1-2; Jeremiah 33:14-16). This is why both Luke and Matthew mention that Jesus was a descendent of David (Matthew 1:1; Luke 3:31). Those who wished to express their belief that Jesus was the promised Messiah used the title Son of David.

Israel had also received many prophetic descriptions of the work that the Messiah would do on earth. Many, of course, expected the Messiah to overthrow Rome and restore Jewish self-determination. Others anticipated a time of peace and justice when Messiah would liberate prisoners and empower the meek (Isaiah 61:1-2). However, the messianic promise that may have most appealed to Bartimaeus was that in this time of restoration, God would open blind eyes (Isaiah 35:5-6; 42:6-7). Somehow, in the midst of overhearing many conversations on the Jericho Road, Bartimaeus had come to the conclusion that Jesus must be the promised Messiah—one able to open the eyes of the blind. This was his chance: "Jesus, Son of David, have mercy upon me!"

Read Matthew 9:27;
12:23; 15:22; 21:9;
22:42; and enough of the
surrounding verses to
understand the context.
How did Jesus respond to
other people who
addressed him using the
title *Son of David*? What
theological belief does the
use of this title reflect?

Recreate the setting for
Bartimaeus and dramatize
it. Assign parts for the
blind man, Jesus, disci-
ples, and the crowd. After
the dramatization, ask:
What was at stake for each
of the participants? What
were the immediate, then
long-range implications of
this successful healing?
What if the persons in the
crowd had prevailed? What
do you think you might
have done had you been
Bartimaeus? someone in
the crowd? a disciple?

Faith and Healing ■

Jesus told Bartimaeus that
his faith made him well. Is
it necessary for the sick
person to have faith before
God will heal him or her?
Why? How is faith revealed
in prayer?

Discuss the connection
between healing and faith
in this Bible passage. If we
consider Bartimaeus's conversation with Jesus to be

In the midst of this noisy crowd, Jesus heard someone call him by a messianic name, *Son of David*. It was the language of faith saying: "I know who you are; you are the One we have been waiting for." Jesus immediately called for him. Was this man just repeating the gossip he had heard or did he *really* understand what he had said?

Bartimaeus threw aside his cloak and jumped to his feet. The cloak is an outer garment that was also used as a blanket or protective covering; according to Exodus 22:26, if taken in pledge, it must be returned to the owner at night. This cloak may have represented the major part of whatever assets Bartimaeus had, yet he threw it aside—a gesture implying that he literally divested himself of whatever encumbrance stood between him and Jesus. This may have been a reckless act, for he had no proof either that he would be healed or that he would get back his cloak. Yet, he showed himself ready to obey and follow. Testing him further, Jesus asked what he wanted. "My teacher [rabbi], let me see again" (10:51). The blind man demonstrated faith in a Messiah he had never seen. Jesus saw his faith and healed his blindness (10:52).

Faith and Healing

In this passage, we see a definite connection between healing and faith. Bartimaeus believed that his healing was possible because the Messiah was present. He believed that the Messiah would be a powerful person, able to open blind eyes. When he made himself known and clearly stated his petition, we could liken it to prayer because he was talking to Jesus. The emphasis here should be placed upon Bartimaeus's belief in Jesus and not the words "Son of David."

The interrelationship between faith and healing is often misunderstood. Healing does not happen magically as a result of speaking the proper words or performing extraordinary acts of faith, such as discontinuing essential medications. Bartimaeus's healing was a gift of God's grace to the faithful, not a product of rituals or faith formulas.

What's in a Name?

Bartimaeus's use of the messianic title calls attention to another prayer concern. What about our use of special phrases, titles, and formulas when we pray? More specifically, what does it mean to pray in the name of Jesus?

Why do we pray in Jesus' name? We pray in Jesus' name because Jesus invited us to do so. Read John 14:12-14; 15:7; 16:23-24. The writer of First John reminds us that God will hear any prayer that is prayed by those who pray according to his will (5:14-15).

Symbolically, what does it mean to pray in Jesus' name? We pray in Jesus' name for at least two reasons. One, knowing another's name was a sign of power. To claim the name of a patron, in this case the Messiah, we place ourselves under his protection and care. Second, we understand that as Christians we are called upon to represent Christ. The apostle Paul spoke of us as ambassadors and ministers of Christ (2 Corinthians 3:5-6; 5:20). When we pray in the name of Jesus, we not only invoke his care but also act on Christ's behalf.

As representatives of the Lord Jesus Christ, we, like the early disciples, have been commissioned and given authority to continue Christ's ministry "in his name." The early church carried this out by continuing the works they had seen in the ministry of

---

representative of prayer, what do we learn about prayer and healing from this passage?

What's in a Name? ■

Read John 14:12-14; 15:7; and John 16:23-24. What does it mean to pray in the name of Jesus? What is the effect? Can a person who has not confessed belief in Jesus Christ rightfully pray in the name of Jesus? Why?

Jesus commissioned the disciples to go out on his behalf (Matthew 10:1; Luke 10:19; Matthew 16:19; John 20:21; Acts 1:8) and Paul referred to the agents of Christ as ambassadors (2 Corinthians 3:6; 5:20). Review these passages; then imagine or dramatize what it means to be an ambassador in the name of Christ. What do these verses imply about our role in the world as representatives of Christ? In what way is every Christian a minister of Christ?

In what symbolic and practical ways do we continue to participate in the healing ministry of Jesus Christ? Take a few moments to make a list or write in a journal some practical ways in which you will look for and try to participate in a healing ministry of some kind.

Examine these Scriptures concerning the power of God and of the Christ. How does it make you feel to know that God is willing to share this power with you personally? Do you personally accept this gift and responsibility? If not, how could you begin? If so, how can you encourage others to do the same?

Consider the model of the early church members in extending themselves in the name of Christ for others. How is their practice a model for you? How do you see yourself as a part of the continuity of Christian "saints" and workers for God?

Examine these passages about the mission of Jesus Christ. In what ways do you feel called to become a part of this mission?

Christ. That commission is still the same, but how we carry it out has been interpreted in different ways. We can look at our commission to do the works that Jesus did in both literal and symbolic terms. For example, Christians may find themselves praying for the sick or working toward healing in our society. Seen symbolically, healing takes the form of healing a city, a family, a nation, an environment, or healing a broken body. We heal in more literal terms when we exercise our own "pastoral care" skills in speaking a consoling word, nursing another who is ill, and caring for our own physical and spiritual well-being.

What happens when we pray in Jesus' name? Christ has unlimited power (Matthew 28:18) and is seated above every other power in the universe (Ephesians 1:17-23). Everything and everyone is subject to him (Philippians 2:9-10; 1 Peter 3:21-22). We do not have the power to bring about the will of God on earth; but the power of God, through Jesus Christ, is more than enough to accomplish any task. When we use the name of Jesus in prayer, we, in essence, are making a declaration that we believe that the power of God is made available for the task, through Jesus Christ. We, like Bartimaeus, also stand ready to act as God's agents in carrying out what God wills.

The early church prayed in the name of Jesus when praying for the mission or purposes of Christ to be fulfilled. They preached to nonbelievers in the name of Jesus (Acts 9:26-29). They baptized new converts and taught them discipleship in the name of Jesus (Matthew 28:19; Acts 2:37-41). People were healed in the name of Jesus (Acts 3:6-10). The early church knew that their power rested in the finished work of

Sing or say together one or more hymns about the power of Jesus' name, such as "All Hail the Power of Jesus' Name," "At the Name of Jesus," "Jesus! the Name High over All," or "Hail to the Lord's Anointed." How does the music influence how you think about, feel about, and experience your participation in the name of Christ?

Jesus Christ, and they acted boldly in the name of Jesus (Mark 16:17-18).

The power of Christ is also made available to us for God's purposes. As we will say a number of times in this volume, Jesus Christ came to earth with a mission. He came to give his life as a ransom for the lost (Mark 10:45). He came for both Jew and Gentile (Matthew 15:24; Luke 2:28-32). He also came to destroy the works of the devil (Hebrews 2:14; 1 John 3:8). When Jesus returned to heaven, he entrusted and directed us to carry out this mission. When we labor for a just and equitable society, both in our own country and abroad, we also are working to destroy the works of evil. When we minister to the homeless and counsel those whose lives have been ravaged by drugs and violence, we are also working to destroy the works of the devil and rightly do so in the name of Jesus.

Christianity has no magic formulas. When we use the name of Jesus, we are not using a special word that is guaranteed to get results. Instead, we use the name of Jesus because we belong to Christ and represent Christ. Christ has been given all power and authority to carry out the will of God on this earth, and we remind all who oppose God's will of that power and authority when we pray in his name.

Read Acts 19:13-20. What happened to the exorcists? Is it possible to suffer ill consequences of using the name of Christ improperly? What would be considered improper? What might be the consequences, if any?

Some Christians are overly careful to say "in the name of Jesus" when they pray, because they believe that just saying the words will guarantee an answer to prayer. In Paul's time, some Jewish exorcists made the mistake of using the name of Jesus as an incantation—to their detriment (Acts 19:13-20). True prayer in the name of Jesus is backed by a faith in Jesus Christ that embraces his identity, his mission, and our relationship to him. Without faith in Jesus, the words themselves are empty and meaningless.

A Paralyzed Man

Read Mark 2:1-12. Form small groups of two or three persons and write a paraphrase of the story, putting it in contemporary terms. Then, either write or take turns telling an extended ending beyond what the Scripture reveals. What happened in the story? What was at stake for each of the participants and observers? With whom did you most closely identify and why? How did the different participants and observers feel and why?

In the extended ending, what happened? Was the ending for each group significantly different? What does your own speculation about what happened afterward reveal about your understanding of Christ and his healing ministry? What does it inspire in you? What are the implications in all this for your own faith community?

Jesus Heals a Paralyzed Man

Early in Jesus' ministry there was an interesting incident that teaches us the importance of our prayers for the sick among us. The Bible describes a man who was paralyzed (Mark 2:1-12), so helpless that four of his friends carried him on a mat. We hear nothing of the man's faith or even of his desire to see Jesus; but his friends took heroic measures to ensure that Jesus was aware of his need. When the crowds prevented these four men from making their way into the house in Capernaum where Jesus was speaking, they climbed up on the roof of that house, tore an opening in the mud-thatch roofing, and lowered their friend down right in front of Jesus (2:4)!

What happens next is telling. The paralyzed man was obviously not one of the faithful who had finally arrived in Jesus' presence but a sinner, because Jesus first forgave him. For some of the scribes who were present, this act of forgiveness created a faith crisis. No one could forgive sins except God (2:7)! Blasphemy, they cried! Jesus responded by healing the paralyzed man, thereby providing proof of his divine status to both the scribes and the man who was sick.

The Importance of Praying

Review this Kansas City prayer experiment. Describe a time when someone else's prayers made a profound difference in your life. Did you know about the prayers

The Importance of Praying for Others

An interesting study was recently published in The Archives of Internal Medicine *(Vol. 159, October 25, 1999). In Kansas City, Missouri, nearly one thousand patients at the Mid-America Heart Institute were divided into two groups. One group received intercessory prayer (someone*

at the time? Are you aware of your own prayers for someone else being effective at a critical time? What happened?

An intercessor is a person who prays for someone else, perhaps without their knowledge. Read Deuteronomy 9:7-29. What *motivated* Moses to pray repeatedly for such difficult people? What *qualified* Moses to intercede for the people of Israel? Why did God *listen* to Moses? What do we learn from this passage about praying for other people?

When Jesus told the paralyzed man that his sins were forgiven, he drew attention to both the man's need for forgiveness and his own authority to forgive sin. What, if anything, is the relationship between illness, sin, forgiveness, and healing? Is it possible to intercede effectively for another person if we do not know what his or her actual needs are? How does the story of the four intercessory friends symbolize both *prayer* and *action*?

Healing, ■ A Kingdom Sign

Form several small groups and divide Matthew 12:38-39; 16:1-4; 24:3, 30; Luke 4:18; John 6:30; Isaiah 29:18-21; 35:4-7; and 61:1-2 among them. Distribute art supplies or use a journal to illustrate

prayed for them) without their knowledge. The prayers of the intercessory group were not directed toward the other group of patients.

The intercessors were a group of 75 volunteers drawn from various denominations in the local community. They prayed daily for the patients for 28 consecutive days asking simply for "a speedy recovery with no complications." None of the patients knew about the study. Yet, at the end of the 28 days, the patients who had been prayed for fared 11 percent better than those who had not received prayer. This study is a powerful, contemporary illustration of the importance of our prayers for others.

Mark tells us that when Jesus saw the faith of the friends (Mark 2:5), he responded to the man's needs. This points clearly to the importance of our prayers for others. This man could go nowhere without assistance. He had friends who cared enough about him to carry him some distance and take drastic measures to ensure that he had an audience with the Great Physician. He was both healed and forgiven because of the initiative of his friends.

Many of us know friends, loved ones, or even distant acquaintances who need our prayers. Some of them, like the paralytic, are unable to initiate fellowship or conversation with God.

Healing, a Sign of the Kingdom of God

Jesus was asked a number of times by his disciples and the religious elite for a sign that he was the Messiah (Matthew 12:38-39; 16:1-4; 24:3; John 6:30). Through the Old Testament prophets, the people of Israel and Judah had come to expect that miraculous healings and other signs would accompany

or write about how signs and symbols announce the Messiah.

What do we learn from these verses about the importance of signs in Jewish culture at the time of Christ? If the Messiah were coming today, what kind of proof would we need in our culture today?

List the signs that were expected to accompany the appearance of the Messiah. If we were to interpret these verses for our times, what would we expect the Messiah to do?

Imagine that you are a panel of inquiry investigating claims that Jesus is the Messiah. Review the evidence (Matthew 4:23; 12:22-24; Luke 7:18-22; 10:1-12; and surrounding verses for the fuller context) and draw up a list of questions and concerns that you would want to address to Jesus and his followers. What would you ask? How would you decide on the authenticity of the answers? What criteria would you use to make a decision?
Now, recognizing that you also are a disciple sent in the power of Jesus Christ to engage in ministry, review some of the history of your forebears in Mark 16:17-20; Acts 5:15-16; 8:5-8; 19:11-12; and

the appearance of their long-awaited Messiah (Isaiah 29:18-21; 35:4-7; 61:1-2).

After his baptism and temptation, Jesus began his ministry with the shocking declaration that he was the fulfillment of Isaiah's prophesy: "The Spirit of the Lord is upon me, / because he has anointed me to bring good news to the poor. / He has sent me to proclaim release to the captives / and recovery of sight to the blind, / to let the oppressed go free, / to proclaim the year of the Lord's favor" (Luke 4:18; see Isaiah 61:1-2).

It was not immediately evident to all that Jesus was the Messiah. Many thought of him as one of the prophets who performed miracles, while his opponents accused him of consorting with devils (Matthew 12:22-24). At first, even John the Baptist was not sure what Jesus was doing and sent messengers to ask questions. In response to their questions, Jesus healed many who were present there and again reminded those messengers of the ministry of the Messiah, which included healing (Luke 7:18-22). Throughout his ministry, Jesus provided the signs and wonders expected of the Messiah. Jesus was known throughout the region for healing every kind of disease imaginable (Matthew 4:23; 9:35).

Near the end of his ministry, Jesus gave the following instructions to seventy (or seventy-seven) of his disciples when he sent them to announce his coming: "Remain in the same house, eating and drinking whatever they provide, for the laborer deserves to be paid. Do not move about from house to house. Whenever you enter a town and its people welcome you, eat what is set before you; cure the sick who are there, and say to them, 'The kingdom of God has come near to you' " (Luke 10:7). From that point, the

1 Corinthians 12. What do we learn from these verses about the ministry of healing in the early church? How might these events have been regarded as a sign of the kingdom of God? How do you feel that you are a part of this ministry (remembering that you are part of a community)? What barriers and opportunities do you find? How do you overcome or take advantage of them?

Prayer, Healing, and Symbolism ■

Use a commentary and study more about the healing of the woman in Mark 5:28. What did she risk in reaching out to touch Jesus? At what risk did she put him? What were the consequences for her in her community because of her illness? What wider implications would her healing have beyond health concerns?

Think about an instance in which illness (of any kind) placed the patient at odds with or on the fringe of the community (as many HIV-positive persons must be, for example). How does ill-

disciples were also known to participate in the healing ministry of Jesus Christ.

After the Resurrection, members of the early church also prayed successfully for healing and pointed to it as one of the signs that the kingdom of God was near. Mark 16:17-20, though not part of many early manuscripts, lists the signs of the kingdom of God that would accompany believers. Some scholars believe it was added to the manuscript by early Christians much as the doxology was added to the Lord's Prayer. This highlights the fact that early Christians considered the healing a sign of the kingdom of God. Healing continued to function as a sign of the Kingdom throughout the historical period covered by the Acts of the Apostles and beyond (Acts 5:14-16; 8:5-8; 19:11-12). The apostle Paul clearly identified healing as one of the spiritual gifts (1 Corinthians 12).

Prayer, Healing, and Symbolism

"For she said, 'If I but touch his clothes, I will be made well' " (Mark 5:28).

Many of us have heard the story of the woman who was healed by touching the hem of Jesus' garment. The faith she demonstrated by touching his outer garment provides a convenient opening for our discussion of prayer, healing, and symbolism. What was it about Jesus' clothes that made the woman feel that they would play an important part in her healing?

The Jews lived with many symbols of their relationship with God and their commitment to keeping God's word. You may be familiar with the Jewish *mezuzah*, the small wooden case containing Scripture, at the doorposts of many Jewish homes (Deuteronomy 11:20). Or, you may have read about a small leather case worn on the head or forearm containing

ness marginalize persons, and what obligation is thus placed on those to whom much grace is shown?

Though Christians do not normally write Scripture on the walls of their homes, in what other ways can we be reminded visually of our faith in God through Christ? List the Christian symbols that remind you of your faith.

Or, walk through your worship space, and later your home, to identify the signs and symbols that remind you of the sacred. In what way do these symbols, spaces, sensory experiences, and the memories they evoke help create a sense of the divine for you?

In small groups, look up the Scriptures in this section that have to do with laying on hands for prayer, healing, blessing, and affirmation in the church. In each group, begin to formulate a ritual or liturgy for community use that includes the laying on of hands for prayer or healing, and so on. Think about the purpose of the liturgy. What music, movement, use of silence, visual aids, and so on might be appropriate.

How does working on a worship experience help you understand the impor-

portions of Scripture to remind the wearer of God's commandments (Deuteronomy 6:8). A blue fringe worn on the border of a garment was yet another of these visual reminders of the wearer's covenant relationship with God. Jesus denounced the Pharisees for enlarging their fringes in order to appear more pious (Matthew 23:5). As a traditional Jewish teacher, Jesus would have worn this fringe on the border of his garment. It was a symbol of the covenant and a sign of his relationship with God.

In churches today, we are surrounded with signs and symbols of our faith. One that immediately comes to mind is the empty cross found in most Protestant Christian churches symbolizing sacrifice, redemption, and Resurrection. The Communion elements and the baptismal font are other powerful symbols of the covenant and grace offered to us by God in the midst of our community.

Prayers for healing are often accompanied with symbols that we have received from both Christ and the early church. For example, when praying for healing, we often lay our hands on the sick person as Jesus did (Mark 6:5; 8:23; Luke 4:40; 13:13). This was a practice continued by the early church (Acts 9:17-18).

When Jesus touched people, it was the same as being touched by God, because he and God are one (John 10:30). When we follow his example by laying our hands on the sick and praying for them, we stand symbolically as God's representatives in the prayer relationship. Our hands are powerless; but we stand as faithful, caring representatives of our powerful Lord, who believe as did Bartimaeus that healing is possible.

tance and transformational character of laying on hands?

Many people are uncomfortable with having another person's hands placed upon them in prayer. What other symbols of the presence of God might be meaningful for such persons?

Pretend that you are preparing to visit several church members who are either homebound or living in nursing homes. Many of them are sick and will expect you to pray for their healing. Write a prayer to use for these visits.

We also follow Jesus' example by laying our hands upon children when they are being blessed (Matthew 19:13-15; Mark 10:13-16; and Luke 18:15-17). We continue in the traditions of the early church by laying our hands upon ministers when they are being affirmed by the church (Acts 13:2-3; 1 Timothy 4:14; 2 Timothy 1:6).

Anointing with oil is another of the symbols used by the early church. In biblical times, olive oil was commonly used as an emollient in healing. When coupled with prayer, anointing with oil served as an outward symbol of the miraculous healing power of God. In Mark 6:13, we see that the early disciples anointed the sick with oil and prayed for them before the crucifixion and resurrection of Christ. After the Resurrection, we read of this practice again in the New Testament when James (5:13-16) says, "Are any among you suffering? They should pray. Are any cheerful? They should sing songs of praise. Are any among you sick? They should call for the elders of the church and have them pray over them, anointing them with oil in the name of the Lord. The prayer of faith will save the sick, and the Lord will raise them up; and anyone who has committed sins will be forgiven. Therefore confess your sins to one another, and pray for one another, so that you may be healed. The prayer of the righteous is powerful and effective."

Jesus and Lazarus

Read John 11:1-44. Though this prayer was directed to God, it was prayed for our benefit. Are there ever times when our public prayers are used for the purpose of teaching those who are present?

Jesus and Lazarus

"Jesus looked upward and said, 'Father, I thank you for having heard me. I knew that you always hear me, but I have said this for the sake of the crowd standing here, so that they may believe that you sent me.' When he had said this, he cried with a loud voice, 'Lazarus, come out!' " (John 11:41b-43).

Mary and Martha originally had asked Jesus to prevent Lazarus's death. What in your opinion enabled them to believe that Jesus could "heal" Lazarus after he was dead and buried? Jesus wept at Lazarus's tomb and considered him a friend. What does it mean to be considered God's friend?

In your opinion, is it easier to pray from the vantage point of being a friend of God or from that of being a servant of God (or does it matter)? Why?

Bible 301 ☐

Distribute copies of your hymnal or worship resources that include various rituals for difficult times, such as a healing service or funeral. Look at the prayers. How do they help us confront the reality of illness or death? illustrate our beliefs in God as the final Healer? bring comfort?

This prayer for the restoration of Lazarus is one of Jesus' prayers prayed for our hearing. He began with a classic Jewish prayer of thanksgiving: "Father, I thank you for having heard me." On at least one other occasion Jesus had broken spontaneously into a prayer of thanksgiving. "I thank you, Father, Lord of heaven and earth, because you have hidden these things from the wise and the intelligent and have revealed them to infants" (Matthew 11:25). The remaining portions of this prayer and the one in John's Gospel, after the thanksgivings, were prayed solely for our benefit. The purpose of the prayer in John was to demonstrate that the coming miracle, raising Lazarus from the dead, was from God.

If we study this prayer, looking only for a model to emulate, we will be sorely disappointed. If, however, we examine the circumstances surrounding this prayer, as we have done in the previous passages, we stand to learn a great deal more.

For example, before this prayer, Jesus wept (John 11:35). Scholars have tried in vain to pinpoint the exact reason for his weeping. Scripture strongly suggests that Jesus wept because Lazarus was his friend and his sisters Mary and Martha were suffering at his death (John 11:1-2, 32-33).

Through Scripture we learn that Mary, Martha, and Lazarus had often shared hospitality with Jesus and his disciples (Luke 10:38-42). They were probably a well-to-do family. John tells us that it was Mary who had anointed Jesus with costly perfume in the home of Simon the Leper when they were present for a dinner in Jesus' honor (John 11:2; see Matthew 26:6-7). This identification is not at all certain, however, especially in light of how the nameless woman is characterized in the parallel accounts in Mark 14:3-9 and Luke 7:36-50. In spite of the fact that Jesus was going to raise him from death, Lazarus's suffering had already caused his friends a great deal of grief.

For us, this is good news because prayer is heavily grounded in our relationship with God, which goes beyond being forgiven for our sins. It extends beyond obedience. Our relationship with God also embraces friendship with God. Abraham was known as the friend of God (Isaiah 41:8; James 2:23). We have also been invited to be friends of God (John 15:13-15).

When we pray, our prayers are not received by a stern judge or an unyielding tyrant who requires spiritual heroics on our part before we can expect an answer. Our prayers are received by our Divine Friend. Because God is our friend, we can always expect to receive a caring response to our prayers. This does not mean that we will always agree with or understand the way that our prayers are answered. It does, however, mean that all of our prayers, including our prayers for healing, are lovingly heard.

Closing Prayer

Sing or say together a hymn / prayer, such as "What a Friend We Have in Jesus," "My Prayer Rises to Heaven," "Dear Lord and Father of Mankind," "Prayer Is the Soul's Sincere Desire," or "Thou Hidden Source of Calm Repose."

Prayers for Next Week

Intercessory prayer does not need to intrude upon the person being prayed for. This week, select one person who could benefit from additional prayer and pray secretly for him or her all week. Make note of the date you begin your intercessions for this person for possible future reference.

The John 17 Prayer

Session Focus ■

This session focuses on Jesus' prayer found in John 17, with particular attention to its prayer themes.

Session Objective ■

The objective of this session is to acquaint the student with some of the issues that Jesus summarized in his prayer with particular emphasis upon the topic of Christian unity.

Session Preparation ■

Have on hand a Bible dictionary and a concordance.

Choose from among these activities and discussion starters to plan your lesson.

Only Found in John's Gospel ■

Look at the list of the disciples found in Matthew 10:1-4 and Luke 6:12-16. Who was the apostle John? What else do we learn about this disciple from the Gospels? Read Mark 3:17; John 13:23; 19:26; 20:2; 21:7.

The prayer recorded in John 17 is sometimes called the *real* Lord's Prayer because many believe it to be a record of the actual prayer that Jesus prayed on the night that he was arrested. In John's Gospel, this prayer is included at the end of the private teachings that Jesus gave his disciples on that night (John 14–16). This prayer was offered before the more private prayer prayed in the garden of Gethsemane, which will be covered in our next chapter.

Only Found in John's Gospel

Why is it that *only* the Gospel of John records this prayer? One answer to this question lies in an understanding of the nature of the fourth Gospel. The Gospel of John was written as late as 30 years after the completion of the Gospels of Matthew, Mark, and Luke. There is no certainty that the Gospel was written by John the apostle; but it has traditionally been attributed to him, and it seems at least to have been written by one who wrote in his name and spirit. By the time John's Gospel was written, it is typically held that the apostle John was the last living of the original twelve disciples. The Gospel itself refers to one who was presumed to have been Jesus' favorite (John 13:23; 19:26; 20:2; 21:7), so the assumption is logically made that this favored one was John. Many believe that John wrote to provide important

List the topics of the three major sections of the prayer. Read through it as an overview; you will consider it in detail through the session.

details about the life of Christ and Christian doctrine that might be lost upon his death.

Most scholars agree that the prayer is divided into three major sections: verses 1-5, 6-19, and 20-26. The first section, verses 1-5, concerns Jesus and his Father. The second section, verses 6-19, focuses more upon the disciples who walked with him. All subsequent disciples, including us, are the topic of the final section, verses 20-26.

A Farewell Discourse ■

If you were to offer a farewell discourse/prayer, to whom would you wish to address it? What important concerns would you want to share? Privately use your journal to write a short prayer.

A Farewell Discourse

"After Jesus had spoken these words, he looked up to heaven and said . . ." (John 17:1a).

The genre of the prayer is that of a Jewish farewell discourse. It can be loosely compared to Jacob's farewell speech before his death (Genesis 49) or Moses' song of farewell and blessings (Deuteronomy 32–33).

This prayer was not a private prayer; it was intended to be heard by others much like the prayer recorded in John 11:42. It was not uncommon for Jewish teachers to break into spontaneous prayer while instructing their disciples. In such an environment, the prayer was considered to be a part of the teaching. In this case, Jesus' instructive prayer can be seen as a last opportunity to reinforce the teachings of his entire ministry.

Jesus' prayer was not private; it was meant to be heard by others. Comment on the use of prayer as a tool for instruction.

The Hour Has Come ■

The Gospel writers only became fully aware of the significance of the life and death of Jesus Christ *after* the Resurrection. Can you identify an event or time period during which you became aware of the significance of the life, death, and resurrection of Jesus

The Hour Has Come

"Father, the hour has come . . ." (John 17:1a).

The Gospels speak of Jesus' awareness of his own impending death *and* of the profound implications that his death would have for humankind. Read, for example, Matthew 17:22-23 or Mark 8:31. In spite of the frequent conversations that Jesus had with his

Christ? How did that awareness influence or transform you?

Read the references in John to Jesus' hour. What do you think he meant? What importance did the timing of certain events and declarations have in Jesus' ministry?

Review Exodus 12 and 2 Chronicles 35:1-19 for two Scripture references to what Passover is and how it is to be observed. What is the role, if any, of the priest in the Passover events recorded there? What is the purpose of offering the lamb and having the meal? How does the celebration of the Passover festival affect, even transform, the community?

Read John 1:29-34. What is John the Baptist's understanding of Jesus as "the Lamb"?

disciples about his own death, they did not fully understand the significance of his death until after the Resurrection (Mark 10:32-34). Thus, when Matthew speaks of the way many Christ-events were fulfillment of Jewish Scripture, he is reflecting upon the theological meaning of Jesus' death. In similar ways, John frequently spoke of Jesus' "hour" (John 7:30; 8:20; 12:23, 27-28) drawing attention to the importance of *timing*, as we consider the death of Christ.

The prayer recorded in John 17 is often called the "High Priestly Prayer." Jesus prayed this prayer the night before the Passover, a time rich with meaning and symbolism. One symbol of the Passover was the offering of a lamb as a sacrifice of thanksgiving for deliverance from slavery in Egypt (Exodus 12). That imagery was also captured by John the Baptist who called Jesus the Lamb of God, the one who would deliver all nations into the Kingdom of righteousness.

On that first Passover, the head of each household or combined household, was to sacrifice a lamb and prepare a special meal. Exodus 12 records the commandment to repeat the Passover event as a perpetual memory. Though the Passover ritual was observed in different ways through the centuries, 2 Chronicles 35:1-19 reports that the Levites slaughtered thousands of lambs and kids for the celebration and that the priests purified the people with the blood of the sacrificed animals, reminiscent of the blood mark on the door frames of the captive Hebrews in Egypt. The Passover setting of this prayer and Jesus' request for the protection and care of all believers captures the spirit of this priestly act in Chronicles.

Bible 301 ☐

Using a Bible dictionary and other study tools, define the ministry of the high priest in the Old Testament. Hebrews 3:1; 4:14; and Hebrews 5:5 refer to the ministry of Christ as that of a high priest. As a high priest, what did Christ do for us?

The Jewish believers and early Gentile believers found the concept of Jesus as the High Priest helpful because it convinced them that there was no further need for animal sacrifices. Of what benefit is it to us to see Jesus Christ as the High Priest?

From this point in your session, be sure to note the verses of John 17, in addition to any other Scriptures, and how they fit the whole of Jesus' prayer.

Jesus as High Priest

In Christian literature, Jesus is frequently called our High Priest (see Hebrews 3:1; 4:14; 5:5; 6:20). This interpretation of Jesus' death became very important for later Jewish believers who needed reassurance that it was no longer necessary for them to observe the system of sacrifices handed down to them by the law. The concept of Jesus as the High Priest of the Christian faith also held significance for early Gentile believers, who often were converts from religious systems where animal or human sacrifices were offered.

Though many of us are far removed from the ritual observances of our ancestors, we, too, can benefit from an understanding that there is nothing we can do to merit favor with God. In Christianity, the emphasis shifts from any of our feeble attempts to please or appease God with ritual activities. The new focus is upon what God has already done for all of us through Christ.

Glorify Your Son!

What does it mean to you to "glorify God"? In practical terms, how does someone glorify God?
Jesus was willing to die a horrific death to save humankind and bring glory to God. Are modern Christians ever called upon to experience suffering in order to bring glory to God? How?

Glorify Your Son!

"Glorify your Son so that the Son may glorify you . . ." (John 17:1b).

In Scripture, the word *glory* is frequently used to describe the splendor, the majesty, the honor, or the praiseworthiness of God. Notice the object of glory in this prayer is not the Son but the Father; all that Jesus is about to do is done with God's glory in mind. Curiously, when Jesus speaks here of glory, it is connected with his forthcoming crucifixion (see also John 13:31-32)—under ordinary conditions hardly a situation bringing honor or praiseworthiness. It is the altruistic nature of Jesus' death that will bring glory to God, not the horrific realities surrounding the actual Crucifixion. Jesus gave his life for humanity's benefit; but the manner in which he died was a scandal that grieved both humankind and God.

This Is Eternal Life

Read John 3:14-16 and John 14:6-9. According to Jesus, how does a person receive eternal life? In practical terms, how can a person come to know God intimately? What has helped you know God more closely? In pairs or small groups, brainstorm the ways, settings, and Christian practices that can, or have, aided your sense of the divine. Tell stories about one of those experiences and how it has affected you. What are the most unusual circumstances identified? How does knowing that something outside the typical Christian practices of prayer and Bible study, for example, help you recognize the myriad ways you can experience God?

This Is Eternal Life

"And this is eternal life, that they may know you, the only true God, and Jesus Christ whom you have sent" (John 17:3).

Jesus came to bring eternal life to all who would believe in him (John 3:14-16; 14:6-9). In this prayer he gives a simple definition of eternal life—knowing the only true God and Jesus Christ, sent by God.

The Wisdom Literature of the Old Testament often encouraged its readers to gain knowledge of God's Word (see, for example, Proverbs 2:1-6; 11:9). The word translated "know" in this passage (John 17:3) is not the word used to mean intellectual knowledge. It is instead the word used for more intimate knowledge as in knowing a person. Jesus is teaching his disciples, through his prayer, that knowing God through Christ was central to having eternal life.

Mission Accomplished

Look up the references in John to Jesus' "works." How would you define *works*? In what ways do you see the works of Jesus today? How do you participate in these works?

Mission Accomplished

"I glorified you on earth by finishing the work that you gave me to do" (John 17:4).

Jesus made frequent reference to the work he was sent to do. (See, for example, John 4:34; 5:36; 14:12-13). As the Word of God made flesh (John 1:14), Jesus "pitched his tent" among us and helped us understand the love and the forgiveness of God. Through his teachings, he taught us how to remain in vital relationship with God. Now, through his death, he would secure eternal life for any who would dare to believe in him. His mission had been to make God known on earth and to secure a place in heaven for those who would believe.

Before the World Existed

Before the World Existed

"So now, Father, glorify me in your own presence with the glory that I had in your presence before the world existed" (John 17:5).

One of the parting gifts to the Christian church from the writings attributed to John was his teaching on the pre-existence of Jesus (see John 1:1-14; 1 John 1:1; and Revelation 13:8). Before humanity was created, Jesus, the Word, existed in God, creating the world and all that is within the universe (Colossians 1:15-17). Jesus was not created; Jesus has always been.

Jesus was aware that he was the Christ; and he was aware of the glory he had before the Incarnation. In this prayer, he prays for the restoration of that glory.

Review the Scriptures in this section. Why is it important to understand that Jesus was not created but has always been in existence?

What portrait of Jesus is emerging? (Consider the images so far: deliverer, revealer of God, high priest, glorified, eternal, pre-existent.) How do you relate to this Jesus? How does he relate to you?

Concerning the Disciples

Concerning the Disciples

Named among Jesus' prayer concerns were the disciples and future Christians. Regardless of whether we realize it, we all influence one another. What prayer concerns do you have for your "disciples"? What prayer concerns do you have for future generations of Christians?

One of the things that I learned as a missionary was the value of restating what appears to be the obvious. Shortly after our arrival in Ghana, we met privately with the chief of one of the villages in the Eastern Region. We exchanged courtesies and told him where we had come from and why we were in Ghana. At the end of our meeting, he invited us to visit him for a festival in his village.

Some weeks later, we went with a friend from that village to visit the chief and enjoy the festival. Once we were there, you would have thought that we had never met the chief because we were presented to the chief *again* in his private chambers with the elders

Using this example from African experience, what did it mean "to know" another person? What does that imply in Middle Eastern thought?

What does Jesus mean when he says about God, "I have made your name known to them?" How did Jesus make God's name *known* in biblical times? How can we come to *know* God's nature today? How does Jesus continue to make God *known* to us?

How have you participated in making God *known* to others?

present. Our close friend, who came from that village, introduced us and reviewed the details of our lives and mission as though the chief had never heard them. Then, an hour or so later, we were presented to the chief *yet again!* Outside at the festival, the elders, speaking aloud as though they were the only ones who knew us, repeated in the hearing of the chief and the villagers all that we had said in our previous conversations with the chief. What appeared, at first glance, to be an exercise in redundancy, actually taught me a lesson in relationship. Before we went to that village, we had only met the chief and our friend. By the end of the festival, however, we had been made known, by our friend, the elders, and the chief himself to the people of an entire village—who to this day consider us their friends.

The middle section of the John 17 prayer is reminiscent of those kinds of presentation speeches and reads almost like a summary report:

"I have made your name known to those whom you gave to me from the world" (John 17:6a). In Middle-Eastern thought, to know a person's name implied that one would also know something about that person's character. Consider, for example, *Jacob*, whose name meant "trickster." After a dramatic change of heart, he was renamed *Israel*, meaning "he strives with God."

In Jewish culture, the work of the Messiah was to make God's name known (see, for example, Hebrews 2:12). By implication, this meant making God's nature known. This is exactly what Jesus did while on earth with us. In two of his letters, the apostle Paul reminds us that Jesus was the *image* of the invisible God—making God known to us by word and deed (2 Corinthians 4:4; Colossians 1:15).

The Betrayal

Imagine that you were one of Jesus' disciples present on the night of his arrest. Consider what you would say to Judas and Peter to try to restore them to Jesus Christ. Write your response to them. After completing your written response, consider writing a similar letter to someone who has betrayed you. You need not send the letter; simply use the letter as a catalyst to pray for the restoration of people who may have caused you harm.

Jesus states that he protected and guarded the disciples while he was with them. From whom and/or what did the disciples need Jesus' protection? From whom and/or what are we in need of Jesus' protection?

Both Judas and Peter betrayed Jesus on the night of Jesus' arrest, yet only Peter was restored. Why? Was Judas predestined to be lost?

Review one or more of these passages that have to do with Peter's denial and

The Betrayal

John reports that Jesus predicted his betrayal (13:18) by quoting Psalm 41:9, "Even my bosom friend in whom I trusted / who ate of my bread, has lifted the heel against me." This psalm has thus been interpreted in retrospect as a prophecy of the betrayal of the Messiah. That perspective is reinforced by Jesus' added comment that this was done "to fulfill the Scripture." When Jesus enacted this verse by giving a morsel of bread to Judas (John 13:26), the betrayal was imminent. John tells us that after Judas received the bread, "Satan entered into him" (13:27) and Jesus urged Judas to "do quickly what [he was] going to do."

John reported this prophecy at the beginning of Jesus' long Passover meal discourse. At the end of his sharing and teaching that evening, Jesus prayed his "High Priestly Prayer," alluding to the betrayal that was to come (17:12); and indeed, it happened in the garden, just after the fellowship meal (18:1-12).

"While I was with them, I protected them in your name that you have given me. I guarded them, and not one of them was lost except the one destined to be lost" (John 17:12). This is an obvious reference to Judas's betrayal.

One of the theological problems often seen in John 17:12 is that of predestination. Was Judas predestined to be lost? If we look again at the night of Jesus' betrayal, we see that at least two of the disciples betrayed him in some way. Judas betrayed him for thirty pieces of silver; then, according to Matthew, repented and hanged himself (27:3-5). By

compare them with what has already been reported about Judas. Was there something qualitatively different about their remorse? about the way each sought to deal with his remorse? How might our own Christian stories be different if we cut ourselves off from our community (as perhaps Judas did) when we were most in need of support and forgiveness?

How is it that Jesus and his disciples, including us, "do not belong to this world"? Do you belong to this world? If so, how and what does that mean in terms of your faithfulness and discipleship? How is it possible for Christians to remain in this world without being squeezed into its mold? What, if anything, might you need to change to live as a faithful witness?

contrast, on the night of Jesus' arrest, Peter, denied the Lord three times. When Peter realized what he had done, he wept in remorse (Matthew 26:69-75; Mark 14:66-72; Luke 22:55-62; John 18:25-27). That night, perhaps both Judas and Peter could have been lost.

I have given them your word, and the world has hated them because they do not belong to the world, just as I do not belong to the world (John 17:14). A number of times before this, Jesus had warned his followers that they would be at odds with the world. They were told to expect persecution because of their association with him (Matthew 10:21-25; Mark 13:12-13). As servants no greater than their master (John 15:18-21), who himself had been misunderstood and persecuted, the disciples could expect tensions with the world as inevitable. Christians live with the contradiction that we do not fit in this world, yet we are not to be taken from it (17:15). Our mission is to remain in this world, without being squeezed into its mold (Romans 12:1-2), as living witnesses of the life and resurrection of Christ.

Intercession

One focus of Jesus' prayer in John 17 is on others. From your congregation, family, and friends, can you identify people who regularly offer intercessory prayers for others? A person once advised, "never pray a prayer that you are not willing to become the answer to." Share your reflections on the relationship between intercession and personal action.

Intercession

Jesus prayed for his disciples. Prayer offered on another person's behalf is *intercession.* The Old Testament is filled with examples of intercessory prayer, such as Abraham's prayer for the people living in Sodom (Genesis 18:17-33) or Moses' repeated prayers for the Israelites in the wilderness (Deuteronomy 9:7-29).

Intercession for the entire nation of Israel was one of the functions of the high priest. This is another reason why the John 17 prayer is frequently called the "High Priestly

Read Genesis 18:17-33 and Deuteronomy 9:7-29. What can be learned about intercession from these two accounts? What role should the church play in intercession for the nation?

Prayer." After the Resurrection, early Christian thought transferred the priest's intercessory role to both Christ and the Holy Spirit (see Romans 8:26-27; Hebrews 4:14-15; 7:24-25). Early Christian literature also spoke of intercession as a continuing ministry of Christ in our lives (Romans 8:34). What kind of things did Jesus pray about in his intercession for the disciples?

That They Be Protected ■

Think about the "disciples" that you identified as people who regularly pray for others. From what do they need protection? From what do you need protection? How is it effected?

That they be protected (John 17:11b, 15). Note that Jesus did not pray for the disciples to escape the troubles of this world; he prayed for them to be protected while they remained here. This petition that the disciples be protected from the evil one is reminiscent of a similar petition in the Lord's Prayer: Deliver us from evil.

That They Be Sanctified ■

Define *sanctification*. What attitudes and/or actions reveal that you are actively involved with the process of sanctification? How does this affect your sense and practice of your own discipleship?

That they be sanctified (17:17). The word *sanctify* in verse 17 is very similar to the word *hallowed* that we encountered in the Lord's Prayer. Both imply being set apart for godly purposes. In this case, the word of God is the truth that would set the disciples apart for God's purposes. The truth of which Jesus speaks is not a subjective truth that often leads people astray, but a *revealed* truth that comes from the written Word of God and the Spirit of God, who is also known as the Spirit of Truth (see John 14:17; 15:26; 16:13; 1 John 4:6).

That They May Be One ■

Recount a time when you felt most unified with God. What kinds of activities do you participate in that reinforce your awareness of being "one with God"?

That they may be one (17:22-24). Finally, Jesus prayed for Christian unity. In this passage, *unity* is defined by example, "So that they may be one, as we are one . . ." (17:22). On the surface, the unity of Jesus and his Father at that moment looked more like disunity. God was in heaven; Jesus was on earth. Jesus, while divine, had voluntarily accepted the limitations of also being human. The

The early church had problems conceptualizing their unity in the face of pervasive diversity. In contemporary society, the differences in theological beliefs, economic class, gender, and ethnicity within Christianity pose similar challenges. How then can Christians become one?

What are the prevailing concerns that make it challenging "to be one" with other Christians in your community? Through what means does your local congregation encourage unity within the Christian community in your area?

Read and discuss the meaning of Ephesians 4:5 and Galatians 3:28. What attitudes and behaviors do these passages challenge us to change? How might contemporary church culture be changed if the practice of unity were made a priority? Consider the quotes from Castro and Smith. How do our biases and/or a concept of "remnant theology" affect a desire for Christian unity? How do they work toward Christian unity? What are the values of embracing diversity as an element of Christian unity? Are there dangers? How do you think God is calling the church, including you, to work for the Kingdom?

Almighty God is without limitations. At this moment, Jesus was fulfilling his function as our Redeemer; while his Father was seen as our Creator. Yet, they remained perfectly unified in purpose—the redemption of humankind. Just as Jesus and the Father were unified in purpose, though differing in function, we Christians as diverse as we appear to be, are united by the same purpose.

It appears that the early church had trouble conceptualizing their unity in the face of so much disharmony. The church began as a sect of Jews who believed that Jesus was their Messiah, or Christ. Once the inevitable persecution began, they scattered, taking their message with them. In their travels, the Samaritans, long considered their inferiors, heard and believed their message and were received into the church. Before long, even the Gentiles, once considered outside of the circle of faith, were included in their numbers.

These and other realities caused New Testament writers to stress the importance of Christianity: "One lord, one faith, one baptism" (Ephesians 4:5); You are no longer male or female, Jew or Greek, slave or free; all are one in Christ Jesus (see Galatians 3:28). The mission and ministry of Christians is to encourage others to believe through our word and through our lives (John 17:20). The success of the church's mission is dependent upon Christian unity.

In spite of Jesus' prayers for Christian unity, the one thing about Christians that non-Christians often criticize is our perceived lack of unity. In many ways, we are guilty as charged, judging by the way we tend to see ourselves in terms of isolated, fragmented groups within the body of Christ. Theologian Emelio Castro has suggested in his work, *When We Pray Together,* that each one of us has our own model of perfection in mind when we pray for Christian unity—usually biased by our preferred Christian traditions. Theologian Luther E. Smith suggests that Christian unity is further hindered by what some call "remnant theology." Remnant theology stresses the righteousness of only a select group. This, in turn, causes interaction with others who may be different either culturally or doctrinally to be regarded as a "polluting" experience.

In a world where so many of us cling to rugged individualism like a prized possession, how can the modern church experience unity? To begin with, it is important that we acknowledge that Christian unity does not mean that we will not have cultural diversity or doctrinal differences. Says Emelio Castro, "Particularity does not, in itself, contradict unity, but is the very element of unity." The churches that emerged in Jerusalem differed in many ways from those that emerged in Rome, in Northern Africa, or in India. Yet, they were unified in purpose; all agreed upon one thing—making Christ known.

A Vision of Fulfillment ■

For what reason did Jesus pray that we might be one?

A Vision of Fulfillment

Jesus held a vision of Christians to come, and of our love and unity. We were numbered among those whose future belief in Christ was anticipated. Again, Jesus prayed that we may be one "so that the world may believe that you have sent me" (John 17:21).

We in the family of God are more dependent upon one another than we may realize. We, as Christians, could easily adopt the African affirmation: "I am because we are," popularized by Kenyan theologian John Mbiti. In essence, he was saying apart from one another we have no identity.

Discuss the implications of the Lakota greeting, "We are all relatives here," if it were adopted as the norm for a local congregation.

Closing Prayer ■

Gracious God, We confess that we are often more *untied* than we are *united*. In spite of your prayers for us, we remain divided and are often unaware of the walls that continue to separate us. Sensitize us to our need to come together with all members of the Body of Christ, so that we, together, might bring you glory. Amen.

Prayers for Next Week ■

Consider one or both of the following prayer exercises.

What major concerns did Jesus pray about in John 17? What most impressed you about his prayer? When you pray, what regularly are your areas of concern? After reading John 17, can you identify additional areas that should be added to your prayers?

Using your responses to the questions above, construct a "prayer sheet" containing the major concerns about which you need to pray. Use your "prayer sheet" daily this week as a tool for broadening your prayer focus.

It is said that the Lakota elders of North America open many of their gatherings with a greeting that translates as "we are all relatives here." It is a statement that reinforces mutuality and equality. It is also said that the Lakota people are taught by generations past to build a world for the next seven generations. In similar ways, we Christians also are all relatives here on earth, building an impression of God and the church that will live far past our years.

Prayer in the Garden of Gethsemane

Session Focus ■
The focus of this session is the agonizing prayer Jesus prayed in the garden of Gethsemane on the night that he was betrayed and arrested.

Session Objective ■
The objective of this session is to learn more through our study of Jesus' prayer in the garden of Gethsemane about the natural roles that struggle and suffering play in the lives of Christians.

Session Preparation ■
Have on hand a Bible atlas, Bible dictionary, several basins, cloths and towels for a footwashing ceremony, and hymnals.

Choose from among these activities and discussion starters to plan your lesson.

Context ■
Review John's Gospel and one or more of the other Gospel reports on the celebration of the Passover with Jesus.

Throughout his earthly ministry, we see both the compassionate human nature of Jesus, and the divine nature of Jesus working together to minister to the needs of the women and children as well as the sick and tormented people around him. Jesus repeatedly responded to human need with compassion and acted on our behalf with divine power. He is the God-Man, with emphasis upon his humanity easily lost in the backwash of our amazement as we see the glory of divine power in action.

Without this agonizing prayer in the garden on the night he was betrayed, we could easily be lured into thinking only of Jesus as pure divinity who condescended to live among fallen humanity for a short time. It is here, in the garden of Gethsemane, that we are allowed to see the fullness of Jesus' humanity.

Context

The prayer takes place after Jesus and his disciples celebrated the Last Supper on what we observe as Maundy Thursday during Holy Week. On that fated day, Jesus and his disciples went to a borrowed upstairs room in Jerusalem to celebrate the yearly Passover. (Read Matthew 26:20-29; Mark 14:17-25; Luke 22:14-23, 31-34; or John 13:1-30.)

List the major events re-enacted during the Passover. Discuss the significance of re-enacting the Passover using the lamb without blemish, the blood, and the Passover meal. Why is it important to understand the significance of the Passover in the context of Jesus' prayer in the garden of Gethsemane? What Passover concepts or symbols continue to hold relevance for the Christian church? Only John includes the footwashing ceremony. Break into groups of four. Have large basins, cloths, and towels available. Wash each other's feet, talking about what this act meant for Jesus and his disciples, then for you.

Invite stories from anyone who has participated in a Seder meal. Or, invite a local rabbi to visit and discuss with you the symbolic and spiritual meaning of the meal.

The Mount of Olives ■

Why do you think Jesus chose to pray in one of the gardens on the Mount of Olives rather than somewhere within Jerusalem, the Holy City? Have you established a favorite "meeting place" with God for prayer? How does it help you sense

---

The Passover is an annual Jewish festival commemorating God's deliverance of the Israelites from Egyptian slavery. The Israelites were commanded to re-enact the events that led to their freedom. At dusk on the fourteenth day of the Jewish month of Nisan, a year-old male lamb, without deformities, was killed for each household. On the first Passover, its blood was applied to the doorposts and lintels of the house as a sign for God to pass by and spare the firstborn. Finally, the lamb was roasted and served to the household as part of the Passover meal.

The typical Passover meal makes use of symbols, in addition to the blood of the lamb, that dramatize Israel's deliverance from slavery in Egypt. The lamb, of course, recalls how God saved the Hebrews from death. Unleavened bread is used to call attention to the haste with which they departed. Leafy greens are dipped in salt to remember their tears. Bitter herbs and a number of additional culinary items are used, each bearing its own symbolic meaning.

At the end of the Passover meal, it was customary to sing a hymn. This particular hymn, called the Great Hallel (or Hallelujah, meaning "praise"), was comprised of Psalms 113–118 set to music. Jesus and the remaining eleven disciples sang this hymn and went to the Mount of Olives (Matthew 26:30; Mark 14:26).

The Mount of Olives

The Mount of Olives is located on a ridge one kilometer east of Jerusalem. Jerusalem, considered the holy city of God, was a carefully planned city; and most of its gardens were outside of the city walls. The rabbis cite weeds and the manure that would be used for fertilizer as two of the reasons that having gardens in the city was forbidden.

God's presence or prepare you for prayer?

Bible 301 ☐

As you gather In small groups, divide the Scriptures that mention the Mount of Olives. Using an atlas, locate the Mount and notice its proximity to Jerusalem and the other areas that Jesus traveled. Find other places in the Bible where the Mount of Olives is mentioned.

Trusted Friends ▪

During one of Jesus' most trying times, he invited Peter, James, and John to pray with him. When you are deeply troubled, are you more likely to invite the prayers of others or to pray alone? What are the possible benefits of praying with others? What might discourage some people from inviting friends to pray for or with them?

In pairs or groups of three, invite one member to offer a concern that requires some time for discernment. Do not give advice or attempt to solve anything; rather, ask questions that elicit the points that can be considered. Then pray briefly for God's guidance.

The Garden of Gethsemane ▪

Jesus chose to pray in the garden of Gethsemane. Do you prefer to pray in a certain location or in a certain

Generally, rich persons owned these gardens.

The Mount of Olives is first mentioned in the Bible in 2 Samuel 15:30 when David was fleeing from his son Absalom. In Zechariah 14:4, the Mount is tied to messianic prophecy. It is frequently connected with Jesus' ministry (see John 8:1 and Luke 21:37). It was the ridge from which Jesus rode into Jerusalem on Palm Sunday (Matthew 21:1; Mark 11:1; and Luke 19:37).

In the Company of Trusted Friends

Of the eleven disciples who went to the Mount of Olives with Jesus on the night of his betrayal, only three were asked to accompany him to his favorite prayer spot: Peter, James, and John. It bears noting that a special relationship had developed with these three more than with the remaining disciples. When Jesus entered the home of Jairus for the purpose of raising his daughter from death, only these three men were allowed to go inside with him (Mark 5:37). Later in his ministry, when Jesus appeared in glory on the Mountain of Transfiguration with Moses and Elijah, only these three were present (Matthew 17:1; Mark 9:2). Now, in the hour of his agony, Jesus requested that those disciples closest to him remain awake and in prayer with him: "I am deeply grieved, even to death; remain here and keep awake" (Mark 14:34).

The Garden of Gethsemane

Jesus and his trusted friends went into the garden of Gethsemane. The garden of Gethsemane was located somewhere at the foot of the Mount of Olives, less than a mile from the walls of Jerusalem. The Gospel of John tells us that it was just over the Kidron brook (John 18:1).

posture when you face your most pressing concerns? What is it about this place and/or posture that helps you to pray?

Review the Scriptures that mention the borrowed or offered gifts that aided Jesus' ministry. Imagine what his ministry might have been like had he not benefited from the generosity of his followers.

Bible 301 ☐

Sing or say the words to "In the Garden," "I Stand Amazed in the Presence," or another Holy Week hymn that refers to Jesus praying in the garden. What images do these hymns evoke for you? How do they help you understand what Jesus experienced or how important prayer is, particularly during a time of great need?

A Struggle From Within ■

Why is Jesus' prayer in the garden of Gethsemane so significant and memorable for us? Now consider the gifts and volunteer activities offered by supporters of your church. How would the ministry of your church be affected if these gifts were absent or diminished? What gifts do you offer to the church and, by extension, to Jesus as he struggles to empty himself for you?

The word *Gethsemane* has Hebrew origins and means "olive press." It is assumed that the garden was an orchard where large quantities of olives were grown and pressed into oil, one of the mainstays of Israel's diet.

This particular garden was one of Jesus' customary places of prayer (Luke 22:39). He probably had a standing agreement with its owner to go there as often as he pleased. Jesus was well known in that area and a number of wealthy people supported him financially (Luke 8:3) and allowed him the use of their property and possessions. You may recall his use of a borrowed donkey for his entry into the city of Jerusalem on the day we call Palm Sunday (Matthew 21:2-3), the borrowed upper room just used for this Passover (Mark 14:13-16), and the borrowed tomb that would be given him by Joseph of Arimathea (Matthew 27:60).

Those closest to Jesus knew this as his frequent place of prayer. Unfortunately, this also made it convenient for Judas to lead the Roman soldiers there to capture him later that evening. It was from here, the garden of Gethsemane, that Jesus was arrested and delivered to the Romans to be crucified.

A Struggle From Within

What is it about this prayer in the garden of Gethsemane that makes it so significant and memorable for us? This prayer is a prototype for all of us. If Jesus, who was divine as well as human, struggled to accept and carry out the will of God for his life, it is probable that we will also have to struggle with God's will at times.

It soon became evident to the disciples that Jesus' prayers were different on this evening. Jesus was driven to prayer. He was driven to pray, perhaps no less than he had

How do you normally respond when confronted with distressing personal problems? When facing crucifixion, Jesus was driven to prayer. What actions can we take to develop an "instinct" to pray *first* when we are troubled? If you were to ask someone to help you be accountable to pray when you are most distressed, who would that person be?

Let This Cup Pass ◼

What was the cup that Jesus referred to? What did that cup represent? Have you ever dreaded completing an unpleasant task that you knew would benefit you or others? How did you resolve the conflict that your dread created?

Read Exodus 6:1-13. What do the four cups of wine used in the Passover meal represent? How does the subsequent experience of the disciples parallel that of the Hebrews in Egypt?

In pairs or small groups, recall a moment when you felt you could not take to heart God's mighty promises because of your own "broken spirit." What eventually made you feel otherwise? How do God's promises sustain you in difficult times?

been driven into the wilderness for fasting and prayer at the beginning of his ministry.

Tonight, he was painfully aware that the shadow of the cross hung over his head. Yet, as much as he knew that the cross was his destiny—for at least a moment, he did not want it that way!

Let This Cup Pass From Me . . .

What was the cup that Jesus referred to (Matthew 26:39) and what did it represent? The Old Testament made several references to a cup of wrath that the disobedient would be made to drink (for example, Psalm 75:8; Isaiah 51:17; or Jeremiah 25:15). If this was the symbol to which Jesus referred, drinking this cup would mean assuming the aggregate sin and misery of a world that had responded to God with little besides rebellion and disobedience.

Keeping in mind that this prayer took place on the night when the Passover was celebrated, there are other possible explanations for this cup. The Passover meal uses four cups of wine. Among the interpretations given by the rabbis, the most common is that each cup represents a promise that God made to the Israelites in Exodus 6:6-7: "I will free you. . . . I will deliver you. . . . I will redeem you. . . . I will take you as my people."

If Jesus and his disciples observed the customary rituals of the Passover meal, the breaking of bread would have taken place between the first and second cups. The third cup, representing the redemption of Israel, would have been received at the conclusion of the meal. This third cup is believed to be the same cup that Jesus lifted at the conclusion of the meal and proclaimed the "blood of the covenant" when observing the Last Supper (Matthew 26:28).

Angels in the Garden

Examine the Scripture references listed in this section. According to these passages, what functions did angels serve? Is there reason to believe that the ministry of angels continues today? How do we respond to people who claim to have seen angels?

Not My Will

Read the quote by Julia Esquivel. How do you think a person overcomes the fear of death? How might a person's perspective be affected if death were no longer feared? Do you believe that all Christians should be willing to face the possibility of martyrdom? If you were asked to "come to terms with the will of God for your life," how might you achieve this?

Following the customary ritual, the disciples sang a hymn at the conclusion of their Passover meal. Note that the Gospel writers do *not* record that they drank the customary fourth cup of wine, representing the reign of God, at the conclusion of this hymn. Instead, the Gospels of Matthew and Mark record Jesus' promise that he would not drink the fruit of the vine again until the Kingdom of God had come (Matthew 26:29).

Angels in the Garden

The appearance of angels in the life of Christ makes an interesting study. The angel Gabriel informed Mary that Jesus would be conceived (Luke 1:26-38). Angels announced his birth (Luke 2:8-15). Angels warned his earthly father, Joseph (Matthew 1:20; 2:13). Angels ministered to Jesus when he was being tempted in the wilderness (Matthew 4:11; Mark 1:13). Finally, near the end of this prayer, an angel came to Jesus' side to strengthen him (Luke 22:43). It is interesting to note that this verse and the following, which describes his sweat as great drops like blood, are not included in several of the ancient manuscripts.

Not My Will . . . but Yours

Julia Esquivel, a Guatemalan woman, wrote, "I am no longer afraid of death; / I know well / its dark and cold corridors / leading to life. / I am afraid rather of that life / which does not come out of death / which cramps our hands and retards our march. / I am afraid of my fear / and even more of the fear of others, / who do not know where they are going, / who continue clinging / to what they consider to be life / which we know to be death!" (published by the World Council of Churches, January 1988).

As Jesus approached the garden of Gethsemane, he had a clear understanding of his mission on earth. Should we expect clarity of purpose to be one of the results of prayer?

In the garden of Gethsemane, it is clear that Jesus understood that his death was imminent, and he asked that the cup should pass. What do you believe enabled Jesus to continue on despite his impending death?

In practical terms, what does it mean to give yourself over to the will and plan of God?

Bible 301 ☐

Sing or say together the first two stanzas of the hymn, "Go to Dark Gethsemane." How does this hymn capture the interior struggle of Jesus? How can we "learn of Jesus Christ to pray"?

Do you agree with Howard Thurman's comment that God's will is not our antagonist? If you agree that God's will for your life is best, what prevents you from voluntarily yielding to God's will and agreeing with God's plan for you?

Jesus knew that he had a mission to accomplish. For months, he had been teaching his disciples that he would be handed over to the Romans and crucified. There were no ambiguities; the end was certain. With each telling of the story came the reminder that death would not have the final word; Jesus would rise again (Matthew 16:21; Mark 8:31; Luke 9:21-22). In spite of his sorrow or awareness of the betrayal that would take place within minutes in that very garden, Jesus had a mission that involved his own death.

To place all of our focus on the fact that even Jesus struggled with the will of God and needed to pray repeatedly about this places us in danger of missing its beautiful conclusion. The good news is that Jesus came to terms with the will of God for his life on the night before he was crucified: "Yet, not my will but yours be done" (Luke 22:42).

How do we describe what happened? Richard Foster, writing in *Prayer, Finding the Heart's True Home* (HarperCollins, 1992) suggests that we look at the Gethsemane prayer as an expression of relinquishment where struggle ceased and yielding to the will of God took place. Jesus did not give *in* or give *up*; he gave himself *over* to the will and the plan of God. Any suggestion that Jesus gave in to something he could no longer resist diverts our focus from the mission that Christ had always known—to be the Lamb of God, who takes away the sin of the world (John 1:29).

Howard Thurman, writing in *Deep Is the Hunger* (Friends United Press, 1990) suggests that the will of God is not our antagonist, against which we struggle, or a grand invasion of our spirit. Voluntarily yielding to

Review Matthew 26:36-46 and John 12:27-28. Recall other instances in which Jesus' hour had not yet come. Now, Jesus says, it is time; the culmination of his ministry is imminent, which has both an immediate and an eschatological import. How did Jesus face this time? How do you understand his comment about willing spirit and weak flesh?

How do you face this time? What would you identify as your God-given purpose? How does your understanding of this purpose strengthen your "flesh and spirit," shape your spiritual life, and direct your actions?

In the School of Struggle

What can we learn about ourselves by reading about Jesus' agonizing prayer in the garden of Gethsemane?

Is struggling an inevitable and/or legitimate part of prayer? If so, how should we respond during such times?

the will of God is, instead, our agreement with God's plan for us, which wells up from deep within the mind and spirit. Jesus' words in John 12:27 highlight the important relationship between faith and remembrance: "Now my soul is troubled. And, what should I say—'Father, save me from this hour'? No, it is for this reason that I have come to this hour. Father, glorify your name" (John 12:27-28). In his most intense time of struggle, Jesus remembered why he had come into the world in the first place—to save us.

The prayer in the garden is vastly different from the Temptation in the wilderness. Nowhere in this prayer do we see Jesus petitioning to do something else with his life. What we do see is that Jesus, the God-Man, struggled with real concerns that clouded his vision and obscured his goals for a brief time. He overcame these struggles by remembering his purpose. Perhaps in our own times of struggle, remembering whatever we understand about God's plan for our lives will give us strength to face even the most difficult of challenges.

In the School of Struggle

The Bible teaches us at least two important lessons about our own internal struggles through Jesus' agonizing prayer in the garden of Gethsemane. First, we learn that struggle is legitimate and may not be resolved the first time we pray. The Gospel writers reveal that Jesus prayed several times to be spared from the agony of the cross before finally yielding to the will of God (see especially Mark 14:36).

This is encouraging news for those of us who occasionally struggle to either understand or accept the difficulties of life. Paul struggled in a similar way with his "thorn"

Complete the following sentence: "I believe that when I struggle in prayer

_____."

Why would it take faith to continue to wrestle in prayer until we are at peace?

(2 Corinthians 12:6-10). Through this, we learn that our repeated prayers about unnerving situations are not an indication that we do not have faith but rather are signs of faith. It takes faith to continue to wrestle until we are at peace with an unwanted answer to prayer. It is far too easy just to pretend God is silent and follow our own ways.

God's Will and Prayer

God's Will and Prayer

Read the Scriptures in which Jesus promises that prayer will be answered. Compare this with what has been revealed about Jesus' prayer in the garden and with Paul's later experience reported in 2 Corinthians 12:6-10. What does it mean to you to pray in Jesus' name? How can you tell when something is prayed in Jesus' name?

Do you think it is possible to have "legitimate" prayer unanswered because of the evil or malice of someone else, even over the will of God? Consider, for example, that God did not ever wish for the Son to be killed, but that the evil of humankind precipitated the Crucifixion. How do you understand and explain the effect of evil with God's will and the prayers of the faithful?

Jesus obviously agonized over this prayer and thus understands our own occa-

Jesus prayed that his "cup" of agony would be taken from him, and it was not. In addition, Jesus prayed that his will would align with God's will, and it was. We believe, with twenty centuries of hindsight, that God chose to have Jesus move through what had become an inevitable chain of events that would end not with his cruel and torturous crucifixion, but with the good news of his resurrection.

Jesus also taught his followers that "if in my name you ask me for anything, I will do it" (John 14:14; see also Matthew 7:7-11 and Luke 11:9-13). Does this guarantee that every prayer will be answered precisely as one might wish? No, it must align with the will of God through Christ; otherwise, it is not asked "in Jesus' name."

Second, through Jesus' agony in the garden of Gethsemane, we learn that God knows what it is like to feel abandoned in the midst of the worst kind of struggle. Jesus' trusted friends were chosen to accompany him to one of the most difficult prayer times of his life. The Gospel writers reported Jesus' pleadings with God: "Abba, Father, for you all things are possible; remove this cup from me" (Mark 14:36). Luke tells us that

sions of pain in prayer. Do you believe that Jesus Christ can empathize with you in all situations? How does your belief in Jesus' capacity to empathize with you influence your prayer life?

Closing Prayer ■

Thank you, loving God, for allowing us to see a glimpse of your human struggle in the garden of Gethsemane. From the record of your struggles, we gain strength to face our own. Amen.

Prayer for ■ Next Week

Write in your prayer journal about a situation in which you were able to embrace God's will instead of your own will. Describe the process involved in relinquishing your will to God's will. What personal obstacles did you have to overcome? What do you believe might have happened if you had insisted on carrying out your will? What was the final outcome of following God's will? How can you use this experience as encouragement the next time you struggle to surrender to God's will?

Jesus' prayers were so intense that his sweat was like drops of blood falling to the ground (22:44). Yet, the three men who were closest to Jesus did not share in this intensity; they repeatedly fell asleep, not once, but *three* times! (Matthew 26:44-45; Mark 14:41).

We may never know, for certain, what exactly was in Jesus' mind as he contemplated the cross. Obviously he knew that such a death was particularly painful, sometimes taking days. Some believe that it was the fear of literal death; others that it was the ignominy of dying as a common criminal. Still others have pointed to the enormous weight of responsibility involved in dying altruistically for all of humankind. What we do know, however, is that Jesus did indeed struggle with the decision to endure the cross and that not even his friends were able to support him fully in that intense struggle—they slept while Jesus prayed.

Session Eight

Prayers on the Cross

Session Focus ■
This section's focus is the last four prayers that Jesus prayed on the cross.

Session Objective ■
The objective of this lesson is to learn what Jesus taught by word and example in his last four prayers on the cross.

Session Preparation ■
Have on hand a Bible dictionary, hymnals, and writing materials.

Choose from among these activities and discussion starters to plan your lesson.

Father, Forgive Them . . . ■
Read Luke 23:32-43. What do you believe Jesus meant when he said, "Father forgive them; *for they do not know what they are doing* . . . "? Is it possible to commit a sin without knowing what you have done? What inner struggles would you have to overcome in order to pray for the forgiveness of people who were about to take your life?

Of the final seven sayings on the cross, four of them could be called prayers. The prayers that Jesus prayed in the hearing of others were often more than personal petitions to God; they were teaching moments. The last four prayers on the cross provided a final opportunity for Jesus to reinforce the essence of what he had been trying to teach humankind for the past three years. What spiritual principles did Jesus choose to reinforce in his final prayers?

Father, Forgive Them
"When they came to the place that is called The Skull, they crucified Jesus there with the criminals, one on his right and one on his left. Then Jesus said, 'Father, forgive them; for they do not know what they are doing.' And they cast lots to divide his clothing" (Luke 23:33-34).

In a culture where suffering is often sanitized or allegorized, it is possible to lose the weight of Jesus' words of forgiveness from the cross. Crucifixion was an inhumane form of punishment that had been in use for hundreds of years. The person sentenced to death was physically nailed to a wooden cross and hung outside to die a slow and torturous death. Spectators were usually there—members of the family or perhaps those who had suffered injustice at the hands of the criminal. Wild dogs were there, attracted by the

Research crucifixion *in a Bible dictionary, including the medical details of how death occurs. Considering the strain on the lungs and diaphragm and the sheer pain, speaking must have been quite difficult; yet all three persons spoke. What does this tell you about the importance to the speaker of what he said? Try to imagine yourself in a painful, difficult situation. What would you make the effort to try to say and to whom?*

scent of fresh blood. For some, death took days; for others, it was a welcome gift that came quickly.

The Gospels provide great detail about the crucifixion of Jesus. He was nailed to the cross as others had been and hanged between two criminals, one on his right and one on his left. The criminals on the other two crosses are often called thieves in older Bible translations. Modern scholarship, however, suggests that those being crucified with Jesus may not have just been common thieves but also may have been punished for political crimes against Rome. In a day and time when Herod was the puppet king of the Jews endorsed by their Roman oppressors, the inscription hanging over Jesus' head, "This is the King of the Jews" (23:38) also suggested that Jesus was being crucified for political reasons.

Forgive Whom? ▪

Who were the main figures in Jesus' crucifixion? For whom was Jesus praying? For what does contemporary society need Christ's forgiveness?

Privately in your journal or with one partner, consider someone with whom you need to be reconciled. Write out or tell about your "deathbed" wish for restoration. How might you go about effecting that reconciliation while you can?

Forgive Whom?

For whom was Jesus praying? Any number of people could have been the object of Jesus' prayers. He could have been praying for the Roman soldier who had just minutes before nailed him to the cross. The prayer could have been an intercession for the other criminals who ridiculed him. Or, could they have been for Judas who betrayed him? At a deeper level, were these prayers for the Jews, to whom he was sent and who failed to recognize their messiah? Or, were Jesus' prayers for all of humanity who had failed to realize that God had "pitched his tent" among us?

Forgive . . . ▪

Since Jesus was falsely tried and sentenced to die by crucifixion, he was the victim of injustice. Before even *considering*

Forgive . . .

As stated in Chapter Three of this study book, forgiveness in Jewish culture went beyond mere lip service. According to Jewish custom, a person did not merit forgiveness

forgiveness, what, according to Jewish custom, should Jesus have expected from those responsible for his crucifixion?

Bible 301 ☐

Sing or read together the hymn, "Ah, Holy Jesus." What are the important theological points of this hymn? Do you feel that you personally, or as part of the faith community, have any responsibility in the Crucifixion? In what way, if any, are you like either one of the thieves? For what "crucifying" act do you need forgiveness?

Review Luke 23:39-43. Who of your companions in Christ best follows Jesus' example of forgiveness and generosity and, thus, models grace for you? Have you ever discussed with him or her what that gift means to you? How might you have the opportunity to convey a word of appreciation?

until he or she had *demonstrated* remorse and repentance. Only after this had been done was the person who had been wronged under any obligation to *consider* releasing any claims they had against the offender.

It is here that the magnanimity of God's forgiveness through Christ becomes evident. No one had asked for Jesus' forgiveness at this point—not Judas, not Peter who had denied him, not the Roman soldier who had nailed his innocent hands and feet to the cross. No official representative from Rome, from the Sanhedrin, from the crowd, or even from among his friends had whispered words of regret to him. Yet, as Isaiah had said in his prophecy of the Suffering Servant years before this event took place, he was "numbered with the transgressors" and "bore the sins of many, / and made intercession for the transgressors" (Isaiah 53:12). At this point, we hear echoes of Paul's words: "While we still were sinners, Christ died for us" (Romans 5:8).

In forgiving the unforgivable before he was even asked, Jesus set an important example for us. He had been teaching forgiveness throughout his ministry. From the Sermon on the Mount until the very end of his ministry, Jesus had stressed the importance of praying for our enemies and even blessing those who curse us. Now, at the end of his earthly ministry, at a time when many would have cursed and fought back, Jesus' instinctive response was to pray for those who had wronged him. He provided us with yet another example of God's intentions to forgive us when he forgave the thief hanging on the cross beside him (Luke 23:43).

Several years later, when Stephen was stoned publicly for his faith in Jesus Christ, we see him following Jesus' example (Acts

Compare Acts 7:54-60 with Luke 23:39-42. What lessons about forgiveness can we learn from observing Jesus and Stephen in these scenes just before their deaths? For what ultimate purpose do you believe Jesus offered forgiveness to his enemies? In more recent history, Dr. Martin Luther King, Jr. considered forgiveness a moral imperative. For what possible reasons do you believe Dr. King understood forgiveness as a moral imperative?

In what ways does forgiveness help the victim who forgives his or her enemy? If you were victimized and chose to forgive your oppressor, what would you hope would result from your act of forgiveness? What are some of the detrimental results of *not* forgiving others?

Why Have You Forsaken Me?

Read Matthew 27:45-54. What was Jesus experiencing, perceived or actual abandonment by God? What can we learn from this passage that may help us if we feel abandoned by God?

What do you believe the darkness symbolized on the day of the Crucifixion?

7:60). Nearly two thousand years later, we found the followers of Dr. Martin Luther King, Jr. attempting to follow Jesus' example. When, beaten, hosed, bitten by dogs, killed, ridiculed, and reviled, the early members of the Civil Rights Movement in America considered forgiveness a moral imperative.

True forgiveness helps those who are wrongly oppressed maintain moral credibility. History has demonstrated how easy it is to slaughter those whose humanity has become obscured by their ill deeds. To justify hatred and retaliation against those who oppress or exploit us makes any of us vulnerable to the sin of selectively disregarding the value of *some* human lives. When we provide ourselves with a new standard of measuring the importance of life, it is but a short leap to the mass murder of the Crusades, the horrors of the institution of slavery, or the genocide of the Holocaust. On the cross, Jesus taught us the value of all human life. He prayed for the Jews and the Gentiles who placed him on that cross, before either knew to ask for his forgiveness.

Why Have You Forsaken Me?
"From noon on, darkness came over the whole land until three in the afternoon. And about three o'clock Jesus cried with a loud voice, 'Eli, Eli, lema sabachthani?' that is, 'My God, my God, why have you forsaken me?' " (Matthew 27:45-46).

The trial before Pilate had taken place at approximately 6 A.M. that morning. The actual crucifixion began at 9 A.M. By noon, the Gospel writers report, darkness covered the entire land. The darkness spoken of here was not the result of a natural occurrence like a solar eclipse. This was the eve of the

Passover, and Passovers were celebrated at the full moon, when the moon would have been opposite the sun. The darkness that accompanied the Crucifixion was more like the darkness of the ninth plague in Exodus 10:21, a poetic darkness sent from God defying explanation.

Calling for Elijah? ▪

Why did some people think that Jesus was calling for Elijah? According to Jewish prophetic beliefs, what did the reappearance of Elijah mean?

Read the Scriptures that refer to the coming again of Elijah. Since Jesus was Messiah, how could it be said that Elijah had reappeared, thus fulfilling the prophetic beliefs?

Calling for Elijah?

In the midst of that eerie darkness, we are told that Jesus cried out with a loud voice: *"Eli, Eli, lema sabachthani?"* From this, some of the onlookers thought that Jesus was calling for Elijah. Bible scholars tell us that these words were spoken in Aramaic, which was a local dialect. The Feast of the Passover would have drawn Jews from many parts of the Roman Empire, some of whom spoke neither Hebrew nor Aramaic fluently. Hearing the word *Eli* could have influenced those who did not fully understand Aramaic to mistakenly believe that Jesus was calling for Elijah.

Beyond the language issues, the conversation about Elijah recorded in Matthew 27:47-49 and Mark 15:35-36 is not inconsistent with the context. By this time, a number of people had heard rumors connecting Jesus with the Messiah. According to Jewish prophetic beliefs, the reappearance of Elijah would precede the appearance of the Messiah (Malachi 4:5-6 and Matthew 17:10-12.). Jesus, however, was not calling for Elijah, for the spirit of Elijah had already come in the person of John the Baptist (Matthew 17:13).

To Whom Was Jesus Speaking? ▪

List the prominent theological positions mentioned concerning the question, To whom was Jesus talking? Discuss the implica-

To Whom Was Jesus Speaking?

One of the questions that frequently arises about Jesus' prayers to his Father is this: If Jesus and God are one, to whom was Jesus talking? We understand that the doctrine of the Trinity is at best difficult to explain. The

tions associated with each position. With which of these positions do you agree most? Why?

Jesus prayed for the benefit of his hearers. Is this something that we should do also? What value is there in praying aloud in the presence of others and for their benefit? Jesus also prayed in a language that not everyone understood. Tell stories about having been in a prayer setting when you could not hear or understand the prayer that you knew was being said. How did you feel about that prayer? In what ways can we participate, even if we don't understand?

limited confines of this Bible study only allow us to list several prominent positions that theologians have taken on this hotly debated theological question over the centuries. Some, pointing to the differences in location and function of God the Creator and God the Redeemer, insist that true conversation was taking place at those points. Some traditional interpretations attempt to explain this prayer in particular as a sign of conflict between the divine nature and the human nature of Christ. Others, who prefer to highlight a more seamless relationship within the Trinity, speak of these prayers as an opportunity for us to become privy to a conversation that was going on within God, much like we might think aloud or talk to ourselves.

Most of the prayers that Jesus prayed to God the Father were prayed aloud for our benefit. Jesus specifically indicates, for example, that his prayer before raising Lazarus from death was prayed for our benefit (John 11:42). On other occasions, Jesus burst into spontaneous prayer while in the midst of teaching his disciples other important lessons. See for example, Matthew 11:25-30; John 12:27-30; or even the John 17 prayer.

Feeling Forsaken?

Feeling Forsaken? ■

Read Psalm 22. In times of crisis, are there particular Scripture passages or hymns that you quote from memory? In distressing times, do you find it easier to pray spontaneously or to pray by quoting Scripture, psalms, hymns, creeds, or other Christian literature? What are the benefits of using these theological "tools" in your personal devotions?

The translation of the Aramaic phrase that Jesus spoke on the cross is, "My God, my God, why have you forsaken me?" (Matthew 27:46). Where did these words come from? This phrase is a direct quote from Psalm 22:1; Jesus recited Scripture while he hung on the cross. This is not very different from the experiences of untold numbers of people who quote Psalm 23 when they become aware of their own impending death.

Psalm 22 was an appropriate choice. A

In small groups, read Psalm 22 more carefully, along with Isaiah 52:13–53:12 and the Passion narrative in Matthew 27. Compare them and discuss how the Gospel writers used the similarities to evoke a powerful sense of God's presence and justice in the midst of great suffering and turmoil.

Individually or with one other person, write your own psalm-prayer using an existing psalm as a model. It can be any psalm, such as one of praise or thanksgiving; it does not have to be a lament. Think about how it could also be used liturgically as a psalm *of* the community *in* the community. What universal themes of humankind and of God come through in your psalm? How does it help remind you and the community of the solidarity of the faith community? of the power of God?

number of events in Psalm 22 parallel those of the Crucifixion. For example, the psalm describes the way the soldiers gambled over Jesus' outer garment (Psalm 22:18; Matthew 27:35). The psalmist complains of being mocked and derided (Psalm 22:7; Matthew 27:39), of being parched to the point of death (Psalm 22:15; John 19:28), and of having his antagonists sarcastically suggest that his God should deliver him (Psalm 22:8; Matthew 27:43). The psalm begins by chronicling the suffering of the Messiah, but it concludes on a note of triumph. Though he once felt abandoned (Psalm 22:1-2; Matthew 27:46), the end of the psalm vindicates the messianic figure (Psalm 22:24-31; Isaiah 52:13–53:12). The same person who was once despised (Psalm 22:6), mocked (verse 7), and surrounded by dogs and evildoers (verse 16) will ultimately proclaim God's sovereignty to untold generations (verses 28-31). On Jesus' lips, the words of Psalm 22 became a prayer as well as a demand for vindication and justice. They undoubtedly gave expression to the mosaic of emotions that he experienced on the cross: abandonment and humiliation on one hand and triumph on the other. The Gospel writers, by elevating the parallels of Jesus' experience with the liturgical psalm of lament or complaint, infused their Gospels with the powerful reminder that God is present in the midst of suffering. God is not only present in this suffering but can and will, both presently and eternally, vindicate such suffering, even over the power of death. The use of this psalm is nothing less than a bold claim to embrace the kingdom of God that reigns over all peoples in all circumstances and for all time.

One of the lessons we learn from this particular prayer on the cross is the value of learning Scriptures, psalms, hymns, creeds, or other Christian literature. A prayer does not need to be unique or original to be heard. At times when our own words are inadequate, the words of others in prayer can become a way not only to express our own heartfelt prayers but also to proclaim boldly our faith in a God victorious over all adversity.

It Is Finished

Read John 19:28-30. To what does Jesus refer when he says, "It is finished"? How is the "fullness of time" revealed in the life of Jesus, including the way he prayed?

When some people approach death, they take a mental inventory of their lives. The last prayers that Jesus prayed in John 17, the garden of Gethsemane, and on the cross reveal that a similar activity was taking place. Make a "spiritual timeline" of your life. Include major spiritual milestones on your journey, such as receiving a much-needed answer to prayer, commitments you have made to God, or times when you overcame internal struggle. Reflect on the significance of each milestone. Refer to your "spiritual timeline" throughout the week and pray reflectively over your life. Take note of any benefits that result from this spiritual exercise.

It Is Finished

"When Jesus had received the wine, he said, 'It is finished.' Then he bowed his head and gave up his spirit" (John 19:30).

Dehydration from the loss of blood and from exposure was one of the agonies of crucifixion. Minutes before his death, Jesus received wine for his thirst. According to John's Gospel, this was done to fulfill Scripture (Psalm 69:21; see also 22:15). The sour wine that Jesus received is frequently translated as "vinegar" in other versions of the Bible. He had previously refused wine that had been mingled with gall or myrrh that would have served as a painkiller (Matthew 27:34; Mark 15:23). Throughout the Crucifixion, Jesus was fully awake and fully aware of what was happening. The pain he experienced was real, and he chose to forego anything that would alleviate his suffering.

Matthew, Mark, and Luke record that Jesus cried out with a loud voice before he breathed his last (Matthew 27:50; Mark 15:37; and Luke 23:46). It is believed that the words he shouted were, "It is finished," as recorded in John 19:30. When Jesus said, "It is finished," he was referring to the same mission that he spoke of in the John 17 prayer. Jesus came to redeem fallen humanity and to restore the possibility of our unity and communion with God (see Isaiah 53:10-12;

Read John 10:17-18. What does Jesus mean when he says, "I freely lay down my life. And so I am free to take it up again." Are there ways in which we can lay down our lives for others? that we can take them up again? After laying down our lives, what within us might be different when we choose to take them up again?

What does it mean that Jesus' life was given by him (a gift), not taken from him (an involuntary sacrifice)? What theological power does that gift convey?

Into Your Hands ■

Read Luke 23:44-49. How did the people react when Jesus breathed his last? Share your reflections on why the centurion, the witnesses, and those who knew Jesus reacted in the ways that they did. What is the meaning of Jesus' final prayer, "Father, into your hands I commend my spirit." In what ways do you commend your spirit to God?

Hebrews 9:11-15). Throughout his ministry, Jesus had reminded his followers and his detractors that he had a divine purpose: to work the work of God (John 4:34). At last, everything else necessary for our redemption had been completed. Jesus' hour had come; Scripture would be fulfilled. Now was the time for his death.

At this point, we are reminded of Jesus' words in the discourse concerning the Good Shepherd: "This is why the Father loves me: because I freely lay down my life. And so I am free to take it up again. No one takes it from me. I lay it down of my own free will" (John: 10:17-18, *The Message*, by Eugene Peterson; Nave Press, 1993). In spite of all that evil humankind had done to Jesus, we could not, we did not take his life. He voluntarily laid it down for us and would, within three days' time, take it up again.

The author of Second Timothy, attributed by some to the apostle Paul, prayed in the same spirit when he was aware that he was nearing the end of his ministry (2 Timothy 4:7-8). This kind of prayer provides a vehicle for remembrance. Remembering our history with God is an excellent way to build faith in what God will do in the future.

Into Your Hands I Commend My Spirit

"Then Jesus, crying with a loud voice, said, 'Father, into your hands I commend my spirit.' Having said this, he breathed his last" (Luke 23:46).

Before Jesus bowed his head and breathed his last, he prayed one final prayer: "Father, into your hands I commend my spirit." The words of this prayer were not original; they were a near-direct quote from Psalm 31:5 which says, "Into your hand I commit my

Share any childhood prayers that you may have learned. Which of these are being taught to your children and/or grandchildren? Do you continue to pray any of these prayers today? Have you replaced any of these prayers with others? In your most trying times, what particular prayers come to mind?

Reflect on the impact that offering a daily prayer of commitment to God would have on a person's life.

Closing Prayer ■

Form a prayer circle and ask each person to give their "prayer testimonies," to share what has strengthened them in the past or what they have learned about prayer from this study. After each testimony pray a prayer of blessing.

Close with the following prayer or another of your choosing: "Lord of all Creation, we thank you for inviting us into a lifetime of prayer and relationship with you. Thank you for the instruction and example that Jesus provided in prayer. In the years to come, may prayer become as natural for us as it was for him. Amen."

Future Prayers ■

Review the prayers from this study and identify several aspects of prayer that you have not been using on a regular basis. How can you use these elements to broaden and deepen your prayer life?

spirit; / you have redeemed me, O Lord, faithful God."

Hebrew children were taught to say these words at bedtime much in the same way that we teach our children to pray, "Now I lay me down to sleep; I pray the Lord my soul to keep. . . ."

As a Hebrew child, Jesus had been taught habitually to commit himself to God before drifting into the nightly void of sleep. Now, before walking boldly into the void of death, he committed himself again to God who hears the prayers of both adults and little children. Though the prayer was childlike, it was not childish. It is a clear claim that death will not overcome, a powerful and future-oriented faith in the God of resurrection and eternity and a dramatic departure from the former notions of a bleak Sheol.

The message for us is simple. It only takes a childlike faith to face our greatest challenges, because God—not children; not flawed, human power figures; not ourselves—is in control of us. Once we have developed the habit of committing ourselves prayerfully to God's care, we do not need special words for God to understand what we mean. In times of crisis, when words elude us, it is always safe to return to a familiar prayer—even a prayer that we may have learned as a child. When we pray, God listens more to our hearts than to the actual words that we speak—and God understands what we meant to say.

CPSIA information can be obtained at www.ICGtesting.com
Printed in the USA
LVOW01s0637140114

369344LV00009B/120/P